CATS & KITTENS

CATS &
KITTENS

BARNES & NOBLE BOOKS

NEW YORK

This edition published by Barnes & Noble, Inc.,
by arrangement with Book Sales, Inc.

2004 Barnes & Noble Books

This edition produced for sales in the U.S.A., its
territories, and dependencies only.

M 10 9 8 7 6 5 4 3 2 1

ISBN 0-7607-6224-4

This book was designed and produced by
Quintet Publishing Limited
6 Blundell Street
London N7 9BH

Creative Director: Richard Dewing
Designer: James Lawrence
Senior Editor: Sally Green

Typeset in Great Britain by
Central Southern Typesetters, Eastbourne
Manufactured in Singapore by Eray Scan Pte Ltd.
Printed in Singapore by Star Standard Industries Pte Ltd.

CONTENTS

INTRODUCTION

Cats have been valued and protected and their history recorded since the days of the ancient Egyptians, and although their fortunes have fluctuated from time to time, they have managed to remain virtually unchanged in overall size and basic character.

Today's domestic cat tolerates its relationship with humans and takes advantage of the comforts of a good home environment while retaining its independent nature. The innate behavior patterns of the cat's wild ancestors will exist, even in a highly bred pedigree cat, whose coat and conformation bear little resemblance to them. Even the most pampered of today's pet cats reacts to the thrill of hunting and retains all the physical skills and abilities of its ancestors.

Having a pet cat in the home can be both therapeutic and rewarding. No other pet is as clean and fastidious in its habits, and none is as easy to care for. Every cat is beautiful in its own way, but the wide range of breeds, colors, and varieties of pedigree cats that exists today means all cat lovers can indulge their particular preferences.

The cat is probably the most common domestic animal in most parts of the world. Wherever there are concentrated populations of people, there are groups of cats, either living as feral animals or kept as pets to keep down rodents, insects, or snakes. Yet despite its familiarity with humans, the domestic cat manages to retain its air of mysterious independence.

A paradoxical animal, the cat can be both loving and bold. It combines caution with courage, and alternates periods of total relaxation with those of remarkable agility. It is not difficult to imagine, when watching one's pet cat, its successful little mammalian ancestor *Miacis*, which first evolved during the age of the dinosaurs. Small in build, the cat has always had to rely on skill and speed in order to escape from predators and to catch its own prey. Its specialized dentition in tandem with its retractile claws helped to guarantee its survival as a carnivore during its evolution, and these qualities stand the cat in good stead.

The genetic make-up of the modern domestic cat has been so manipulated by selective breeding that some felines bear little resemblance to those of ancient Egypt's homes and granaries. The noses of Persian cats have been reduced in size, while those of the Orientals have been lengthened. Breeders have selected for heavy bone in some breeds, and for light bone in others. Despite all the efforts to thwart nature, however, the basic structure of the domestic cat has resisted human intervention, and the biology of the animal is the same whether it is a champion Chinchilla or a stray tabby. The great cat-goddess Bast continues to watch over *Felis domesticus*, making sure that all cats remain virtually the same in size and character; affectionate, fastidious felines who

are willing companions, but who will never be subordinate or subservient to humans.

The aim of this book is to show the diverse and interesting range of domestic cat breeds that exists today, exploring conformation, coat types, and patterns. It also examines the breeds' varying care

Even the most sophisticated of today's pedigree cats, like this Abyssinian, retains all of its natural hunting instincts.

requirements and their special characteristics, and provides a brief introduction to the world of showing.

CATS IN HISTORY

Because any pair of domestic cats, from anywhere in the world, will readily interbreed, cats are of a single species, descended from a common ancestor.

Domestication of the cat probably first took place in the Middle East, and the cats encouraged to approach people were almost certainly *Felis lybica*, the African wild cat. This is a lithe animal, very similar to a domestic tabby in color. Many of the skulls from ancient Egyptian cat cemeteries resemble *Felis lybica*, while a small proportion are of cats resembling the jungle cat, *Felis chaus*. It would appear that the ancient Egyptians tamed both types, but the African wild cat was easily the more popular of the two, and probably more amenable to domestication.

Egypt was the greatest grain-growing area of the ancient world, and huge granaries

The cat was deified in ancient Egypt and also used for the protection of the granaries and for wildfowling.

were constructed to store the grain from good harvests for use in leaner years. As rodent controllers, cats must have been vital to the economy of those times. The ancient Egyptians also appreciated the natural link between the cat and the lion, and worshipped the goddess Bast, also called Pasht or Oubasted, who first appeared with the head of a lion, and later with the head of a cat. Bast was seen as a goddess of love, and of the moon. The cat was connected with her as love-goddess because of the animal's natural fecundity, and as moon-goddess because of the varying shape of the pupils of the cat's eyes, which were thought to enlarge and contract with the waxing and waning of the moon. Egyptian statues of Bast show her connection with fertility and pleasure. In several statues, she stands upright, an alert cat's head surmounting a figure holding a sistrum in one hand and a rattle in the other. The rattle symbolized both phallus and womb, and the symbolic fertility of the goddess was further reinforced by several kittens, usually five, sitting at her feet. Women of the period often wore fertility amulets depicting Bast and her feline family.

The original Egyptian name of the cat was *mau*, perhaps from its called of "meow," which also meant "to see." The Egyptians considered that the cat's unblinking gaze gave it powers to seek out truth and to see into the afterlife. Bast, who was sometimes called the Lady of Truth, was therefore used in mummification ceremonies to ensure life after death.

Cats played such a complex and important part in the lives of the ancient Egyptians that the living animals were pampered and in some cases worshipped. After the death of a cat, whole families would go into mourning, and the cat's body was embalmed and placed in a sacred vault. Thousands of mummified cats have been discovered in Egypt, some so well preserved that they have added to our store of knowledge of the earliest domesticated cats.

The custom of keeping cats spread slowly throughout the Middle Eastern countries. A Sanskrit document of 1000 B.C. mentions a

The cat-goddess Bast, with a sistrum, used as a sacred rattle to frighten evil gods, and a small, lion-headed aegis or shield. Both objects serve to protect the litter of kittens sitting at her feet.

pet cat, and the Indian epics *Ramayana* and *Mahabharata*, of about 500 B.C., both contain stories about cats. The Indians at that time worshipped a feline goddess of maternity called Sasti, and for decades Hindus were obliged to take responsibility for feeding at least one cat. Cats reached China around A.D. 400, and in A.D. 595 an empress was recorded as having been bewitched by a cat spirit. By the twelfth century A.D. rich Chinese families kept yellow and white cats known as "lion-cats," which were highly valued as pets. Vermin control was undertaken by longhaired cats, and cats were traded in street markets. Pet cats were introduced into Japan from China in the reign of Emperor Ichi-Jo, who lived from A.D. 986 to 1011. It is recorded that on the tenth day of the fifth moon, the emperor's

A Roman mosaic found in the ruins of Pompeii, dating from the first century B.C., depicts a bright-eyed cat pouncing on its prey.

white cat gave birth to five white kittens, and a nurse was appointed to see that they were brought up as carefully as royal princes. Many legends and stories of cats survive in Japanese literature, the most enduring image being that of the *Maneki-neko*, the listening or beckoning cat, which can still be found in ornaments and amulets today.

Throughout the world, before the witch hunts of the Middle Ages, cats were treated with affection and respect. Their greatest attribute was their superlative efficiency in controlling vermin.

Gods of one religion may become the demons of its successor, and in the case of

nineteenth century, Basque farmers claimed that witches appeared as black cats, which made such animals greatly feared.

Eventually the cat's fortunes turned once more. They became prized possessions, and those with unusual colors and markings were favored as pets. They were carried between the world's continents as precious gifts, and gave rise to the many breeds and varieties that we know today.

Cats eventually gained popularity as pets.

In the Middle Ages, the art of witchcraft was rife. A witch would often have as her "familiar" a black cat, and was said to be able to transform herself into her familiar's form.

the cat, its nocturnal habits, independence, sense of self-preservation, and often erotic behavior accelerated the process during the sixteenth and seventeenth centuries. Witch hunting then reached its climax, and cats figured prominently in most witch trials throughout Europe. Even as late as the

DOMESTICATION

The cat is a mammal—a relatively small class of animals with self-regulating body temperature, hair, and milk-producing mammae in the females. There are about 15,000 species of mammals out of a few million total species of animals.

Following the evolutionary chain that gave rise to all life, the first mammals sprang from reptiles about 200 million years ago. But it was not until about 70 million years ago that the mammals began to assume the dominant role they currently hold. They also began to develop into the many families that exist today.

Several early carnivore (meat-eating) groups arose to fill the niche of hunter, among them the *Miacis*. At first the *Miacis*

The prehistoric skull of the fearsome *Smilodon*, or saber-tooth tiger, an early form of feline that existed until about 13,000 years ago. To accommodate the huge upper canine teeth, which were used to stab prey and then tear it apart, the jaws could open to 90 degrees.

were small, weasel-like animals, but they had the necessary equipment to survive and develop further, while other, competing groups fell into extinction. As the evolutionary processes acted on them, offering them ever wider niches to fill, about 45–50 million years ago they developed into the ancestors of today's carnivore families, including cats.

Spurred on by their hunting prowess, the cats spread quickly and further evolved into many different forms that could best take advantage of localized prey and environment. Few of these evolutionary "experiments" survive today. It has been at least 13,000 years since the saber-tooth tiger—once spread across the globe—has walked the earth. The giant tiger of Asia and the cave lion of Europe are likewise gone, probably becoming extinct even before the saber-tooth.

The first ancestors of the modern cat apparently lived at the same time as these now extinct animals but were better able to take advantage of their situation and continue on. The oldest known fossilized record with a strong similarity to today's cats has been aged at about 12 million years.

As recently as 3 million years ago the earth was shared by many more distinct varieties of cat than the three genera that we recognize today: *Panthera*, the big cats such as lions, which have a small hyoid bone at the base of their tongue that moves about freely and enables them to roar; *Felis*, the smaller cats, which have a rigid hyoid bone and cannot roar; and *Acinonyx*, only the cheetah, which has claws that cannot fully retract.

It is generally agreed that about 40 different species of cat exist today. The domestic cat is just one of them, but with man's help it has developed greater variety than all the others. While coloration and pattern of coat have evolved in wild cats only so far as needed to camouflage them from their prey and their competition, controlled breeding has introduced dramatic variations in the physical features of domestic cats that are totally unrelated to evolution or their environment.

Today's cats are divided into three genera: *Acinonyx* (below), the cheetah, which has claws that cannot be fully retracted; *Felis* (below right), the small cats, including our many domestic breeds; and *Panthera* (right), the great cats, like the lions.

Man has also spread the cat to the few parts of the Earth that Nature had not already taken it. By 2 million years ago, cats had settled on nearly every continent. Continental drift brought North and South America back into contact and gave the southern land mass its first cats. But many islands, such as the Galapagos Group off the coast of South America, had no feline predators until the past few centuries, when man arrived and brought cats with him. These new carnivores meant disaster for the

native wildlife there. Likewise Australia had no cats until man brought them there. Antarctica remains catless.

As man became aware of the value that different animals could have for him, he began to domesticate them. Dogs made excellent hunting partners. Cows provided meat, milk, and labor. Horses were a fine form of transportation.

It was the cats, however, that decided to live with man, not the other way around. What attracted cats to man were the hordes of rats and mice that congregated around the stores of food that man had learned to build up in ancient Egypt. The cats that first chose to live near or with man, and thus became the ancestors of all domestic breeds, were, as

This ancient Egyptian bronze figurine wearing gold earrings was dedicated to the cult of Bast, goddess of fertility and love. The ancient Egyptians were the first to tame the cat. Used at first as a hunter and retriever, it was later valued as a pet, and finally became an object of worship.

we have seen, of the African wild cat species, *Felis lybica*, which still exists today.

The earliest known evidence of a cooperative relationship between man and cat has been dated at 4,500 years ago. It came in the form of cat images painted on tomb walls, carved and molded statues of cats, and even mummified remains of cats.

Egyptian religion included cat images among other sacred symbols even before cats had claimed the granaries as their hunting grounds. They believed that their gods took on the appearance of cats in order to pass down orders and omens. Priests had previously worshipped the lion, but that was a large and dangerous animal. Now, in these smaller, vermin-hunting felines they found a more pleasing symbol. These forerunners of the domestic cat weren't tame, but more manageable than lions.

As each new generation of cat (and there were many under the newly found protection of man) demonstrated greater domestication, the animals came to share the homes of the Egyptians.

Despite their domesticity, they did not lose their sacred status. To kill a cat was a crime punishable by death. The felines were embalmed and mummified when they died, and embalmed mice were placed with them in their tombs. Families mourned the deaths of cats that had shared their homes as they mourned the deaths of human family members. In one ancient city unearthed in the late 1800s, more than 300,000 mummified cat remains were found.

The Greeks were the first Europeans to recognize the mousing value of these

Egyptian felines, and when the Egyptians wouldn't trade any of their sacred cats, the Greeks went ahead and stole several pairs. And the Greeks in their turn gradually sold the offspring of these cats to their traditional trading partners, namely, the Romans, the Gauls, and the Celts.

The vermin-control abilities of the cat continued to be appreciated, and man spread the animal throughout the civilized world, although not without setbacks. It was unfortunate that the Church decided to condemn the rat-killing cat as a pagan symbol during the Middle Ages, as rats were spreading the plague that would eventually kill millions throughout Europe. Persecution of the felines continued to be widespread. The Festival of St. John was annually celebrated with the now unimaginable burning alive of cats in town squares. By 1400 the species was nearly extinct.

It was not until it became apparent that certain physical and mental conditions were not caused by witches that cats began to grow popular once again in Europe.

During the Middle Ages cats were persecuted as agents of Satan, but happily this situation was reversed in the seventeenth century when they achieved new-found respect due to their ability to control plague-bearing rats. By the eighteenth century, cats were highly prized as pets among the European intelligentsia and began to be featured in paintings and literature. This oil painting, *Stable Animals*, is by an anonymous mid-nineteenth-century English artist.

Life is good for the vast majority of domestic cats today, and they are kept as pets in huge numbers all over the world. Ironically, their very popularity as pets has much to do with their independence of spirit and the fact that the wild, "untamed" side of their natures is never far below the surface.

IDENTIFYING CATS

BODY SHAPE

In general shape and overall size, all breeds of domestic cats have retained the same basic structure as their ancestors, unlike dogs, which have been selectively bred to produce very wide variations of shape and height. Cats are, therefore, free from many of the skeletal abnormalities that can affect dogs. Some defects are occasionally encountered, including shortened, bent, or kinked tails, cleft palates, flattened chests, and polydactylism (extra toes). In the main, however, evolution seems to have been particularly kind in designing the cat, proceeding along such a well-ordered path of natural selection that it remains an efficient and perfect carnivore of convenient size, still well capable of hunting and killing small animals and birds.

The cat's frame is designed for fluid, coordinated, and graceful movements at all speeds. Its taut-muscled body and legs enable it to make impressive leaps and bounds. The retractile nature of the sharp claws allows fast sprinting over short distances, holding and gripping of prey, and fast climbing of convenient trees when danger threatens. The cat's brain is large and well-developed, enabling it to assimilate facts rapidly and to react quickly. Its adaptable eyes can cope with extremes of lighting conditions, allowing perfect vision in both bright sunlight and dim twilight. The mobile ears work to catch the faintest sound, and the sensitive nose, allied to the perceptive Jacobson's organ in the mouth, can identify

The Longhaired or Persian body type is large-boned and stocky.

The Shorthair breeds are similar in structure to Persians.

Foreign and Oriental cats are fine-boned and elegant.

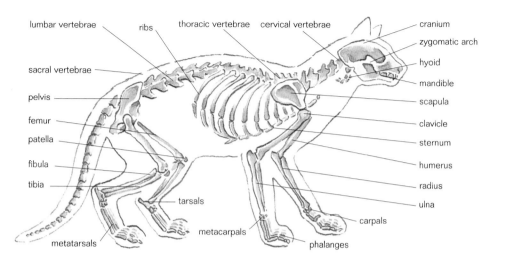

lumbar vertebrae

ribs

thoracic vertebrae

cervical vertebrae

cranium

zygomatic arch

sacral vertebrae

hyoid

mandible

pelvis

scapula

femur

clavicle

patella

sternum

fibula

humerus

tibia

radius

tarsals

ulna

carpals

metacarpals

phalanges

metatarsals

the faintest of scents imperceptible to humans.

Pedigree breeds of domestic cats have been developed to fit certain standards of conformation, color, and coat pattern. This had been done over many generations, with dedicated breeders working out exactly what the desired feline end-product would look like, and setting out to achieve it with careful and selective breeding. Today there are two main types of pedigree cat: those with chunky, heavyweight bodies and large round heads, and a lighter, finer type with lighter bones and longer heads.

Cats of the heavier type come in a wide variety of colors and coat patterns, and they may be longhaired or shorthaired. The former include Persians and similar breeds;

A cat's skeleton consists of approximately 244 bones with discs between the vertebrae as shock-absorbers.

the shorthairs cover cats such as the British, American, European, and Exotic shorthairs. Lightweight cats are more variable in their characteristics. The Orientals, including the distinctive Siamese, are at the furthest extreme from the heavier types, with very fine bone; very long bodies, legs, and tails; long, wedge-shaped heads and large ears. Less extreme are the Foreign Shorthairs and Rex cats, each variety having its own very recognizable features. Some breeds have arisen from mixtures of heavy and lightweight types; these have intermediate features.

HEADS AND EYES

Most cat breeds with heavy conformation, such as the Persian and the Shorthair, have large, round heads, with large, round eyes set wide apart above a short, snub nose on a broad face. The ears are small but have a wide base, and they are placed far apart on the head, complementing the rounded appearance of the skull.

The head of the Longhair or Persian is typically round, with round eyes and full cheeks. The tiny ears set wide apart.

The head of the Shorthair is similar in shape to that of the Persian only when viewed from the front.

Foreign and Oriental cats have long, narrow heads and large ears. Head shape varies in the individual breeds.

In profile, the Persian's head is rather flat. The short snub nose shows a definite "break" at eye level.

Cats of light conformation, such as the Oriental and Foreign Shorthairs, have longer heads of various shapes, and the eye shape varies for each specific breed. Long-coated cats with light conformation have various head and eye shapes, according to the standards laid down by their breed associations.

The profile of a typical Shorthair breed is less flat than that of the Persian with its short, broad nose.

Oriental cats have long, almost Russian noses with no "break" at eye level and a flat forehead.

EYES

Longhaired or Persian cats, as well as most of the Shorthair breeds, have large, round, lustrous eye.

Some breed standards call for oval or almond-shaped eyes, often tilted at the outer edge toward the ears.

Siamese and similar related breeds have eyes of Oriental shape, set slanting toward the outer edge of the ear.

COAT TYPES AND COLORS

Pedigree cats have diverse variations of coat types, ranging from the full and profuse pelt of the Persian to the fine, sleek, and close-lying coats of the Siamese and Orientals. Between the two extremes are the long, soft and silky coats of the longhaired foreign breeds and the thick, dense coats of some of the shorthaired varieties. Some breeds should have "double" coats, with a thick wooly undercoat and a longer, sleeker top coat. The Cornish Rex has a coat devoid of guard hairs, and naturally curled awn and down hairs. The Devon Rex has modified guard, awn, and down hairs, which produce a waxy effect. The Sphynx cat is at the extreme end of the coat-type range, being covered in some parts merely with a fine down.

Persian

Long, soft coat with profuse down hairs nearly as long as the guard hairs, producing a typically long and full coat.

Maine Coon

Long, silky coat, heavier and less uniform than that of the Persian due to less uniform and denser down hairs.

Shorthair

Shorthair coats are very variable, ranging from the British and American breeds to the foreigns.

Sphynx

Apparently hairless, the Sphynx does have a light covering of down hairs on some areas of the body.

Cornish Rex

The tightly curled coat of the Cornish Rex is caused by the absence of guard hairs and short awn hairs.

Devon Rex

Genetically modified guard and awn hairs in this breed closely resemble down hairs.

American Wirehair

Quite different from the two rex coats, the wirehair has crimped awn hairs and waved guard hairs.

Oriental

In the Siamese and Oriental cats, the coat is short, fine, and close-lying, quite different from that of other cats.

The natural color of the domestic cat is tabby. The wild type is ticked tabby or agouti, and the other tabby patterns are mackerel (striped), spotted, and classic (marbled or blotched). The pigment melanin produces black hairs, and most of the self-colored coats seen in cats are produced by the modification of this pigment or by the way in which it is distributed in the individual hair fibers.

Solids

Solid in cat terms refers to the color and not to the build of the cat. Cats of self- or solid-colored breeds must be of a single, solid color throughout, with no pattern, shading, ticking, or other variation at all in color. The most common solid colors cover a very wide range and include black, blue, chocolate, lilac, red, cream, cinnamon, and white.

Black

Blue

Chocolate

Lilac

Red

Cream

Cinnamon

White

Tabby Markings

There are four varieties of tabby patterns, ticked, mackerel, spotted, and classic, which can be found in any of the tabby colors.

Tabby Colors

Tabbies are found in a wide variety of colors, including brown, blue, chocolate, brown patched, blue patched, red, and silver.

Ticked

Mackerel

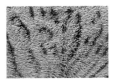

Spotted

Classic

Brown

Blue

Chocolate

Brown Patched

Blue Patched

Red

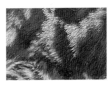

Silver

Abyssinian

Abyssinian cats have coats that are gently shaded, because each hair is lighter at the root and darker at the tip.

Usual

Blue

Sorrel

Fawn

Colored-tip Coats

Coats with the hairs darkening in varying degrees toward the roots are to be found in a number of colors, including black, blue, chocolate, and lilac.

Black Smoke

Blue Smoke

Chocolate Smoke

Lilac Smoke

Chinchilla Silver

Chinchilla Golden

Black-tipped Silver

Blue-tipped Silver

Himalayan

Cats with the Himalayan coat pattern, such as the Siamese, have pale coats with the main color restricted to the head and extremities.

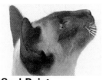

Seal Point

Blue Point

Red Point

Cream Point

Lilac Point

Chocolate Point

Seal Point Tabby

Red Point Tabby

Tonkinese

Tonkinese cats, which are light-phase Burmese cats, show a modified "pointed" effect. The coats are darker than those of cats with true Himalayan coloring, so the "points" are not as dramatic.

Brown

Lilac

Chocolate

Red

Cream

Lilac Tortie

Blue Tortie

Tabby

As every cat lover knows, cats come in coats of many colors in addition to those already described, and most of these are recognized for show purposes in one breed or another.

The tortoiseshells are the most common, but there are endless varieties, including the unusual Mi-ke pattern of the Japanese Bobtail.

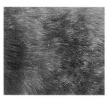

Tortoiseshell

Chocolate Tortoiseshell

Lilac Tortoiseshell

Blue Tortoiseshell

Tortoiseshell and White

Blue Tortoiseshell and White

Mi-ke

CAT BEHAVIOR

Cats are often considered less intelligent than dogs, possibly because they do not respond to training to sit on command and will rarely perform tricks.

It is questionable whether the performance of unnatural actions necessarily equates with a high intelligence quotient, and it may be that the cat is better equipped to channel its brain power into different behavior, such as survival techniques and adapting to environmental change. And could cats perhaps be considered more intelligent than dogs for questioning the reason behind performing tricks, or being obedient to commands?

Young kittens begin to exhibit predatory behavior at about six weeks old. In the wild, the mother cat would bring prey to the kittens. In the domestic situation, a mother cat brings small pieces of meat to the maternity box, making a special encouraging sound to attract her kittens' attention. Mother cats often pat the meat, teaching the kittens to pounce upon it. At this stage of their development, kittens begin to practice hunting movements, crouching down, pouncing, and making mock attacks on their litter mates. Their mother waves her tail, enticing her youngsters to pounce and grasp it.

Adult cats prefer to hunt alone within the confines of their own established territory. Some cats roam long distances from home to visit favorite hunting grounds, and, very occasionally, cats from the same family learn to hunt cooperatively. Acute hearing and excellent vision in dim light

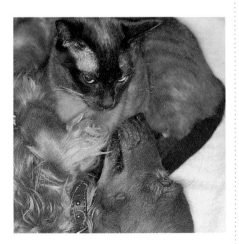

Although cats and dogs get along well together as family pets, it is sometimes difficult for them to understand one another's body language and play behavior.

enable cats to become efficient, silent hunters. A cat often lies in ambush, waiting with infinite patience for its victim to emerge from its place of refuge. The cat attacks in a swift bounding leap, grasping its prey with extended claws, and killing with a lethal bite to the creature's neck. Hungry cats dispatch their prey quite quickly, but well-fed cats, highly stimulated by the excitement of stalking and capture, often play with the prey for some time before finally dispatching it. Playing with prey gives the cats the opportunity to practice their trapping techniques.

Despite centuries of domestication, most cats will hunt, given the chance. If you keep pet cats entirely indoors, you should compensate for their loss of hunting opportunities by providing lots of toys, and encouraging them to play chasing, pouncing, and catching games. Such stimulation and exercise keeps them fit, stops them from getting too fat, and may help to guarantee their survival if they get lost.

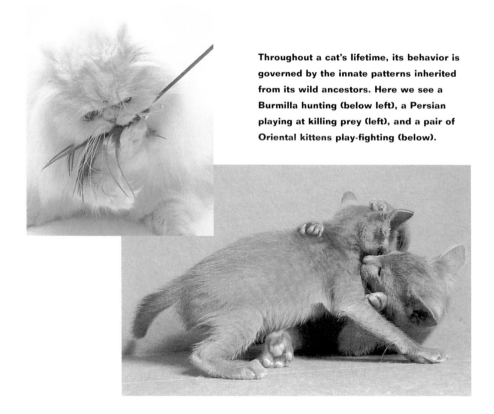

Throughout a cat's lifetime, its behavior is governed by the innate patterns inherited from its wild ancestors. Here we see a Burmilla hunting (below left), a Persian playing at killing prey (left), and a pair of Oriental kittens play-fighting (below).

SELF-GROOMING

It's easy to see how cats acquired their reputation for cleanliness—they spend up to a third of their waking hours grooming themselves. To facilitate this, your cat's barbed tongue can reach almost every part of its body. The forepaws and teeth are also used as cleaning instruments.

Grooming does more than just clean the fur; it also keeps the coat soft and glossy, removes loose and dead hair and skin as well as debris and parasites, tones muscles, and stimulates blood circulation and new growth.

Grooming also has a nutritional function. It provides vitamin D, which is produced on the fur by sunlight, and in hot weather, saliva licked onto the fur performs the same function as sweat, controlling body temperature by evaporation. This explains why cats groom more in warm weather and after periods of play, hunting, or other activity. Cats also groom when they become anxious because it helps them relieve tension and relaxes them.

Cats occasionally groom each other—a useful way of getting to those inaccessible places, such as behind the ears. Mutual grooming is also a sign of a close bond between cats that share a common territory.

loss, or development of furballs. Fur is ingested naturally as the cat grooms, but too much grooming causes the mucus in the cat's body to clump the hairs together, resulting in masses that obstruct bowels and interfere with digestive functions. Many cats regurgitate these dark masses of fur automatically (eating grass helps). If yours doesn't, you'll have to purchase a furball cure or give the cat mineral oil to soften the furball and allow it to pass.

At the other extreme, some cats show little interest in grooming. If yours isn't interested, even after contact with dust, dirt, or plant burrs, try smearing some butter on its fur. If even that doesn't do it, you'll have to do more than your share of the grooming.

Feline mothers are very good teachers, and grooming is one of the first activities kittens learn. The bond between mother and kitten is reinforced during grooming sessions and appears to give mutual pleasure.

Mutual grooming is also normal in healthy cats. It carries over from the days when the mother groomed the kittens, reinforcing her bond with them and showing them how they could lick each other, especially in hard-to-reach areas like behind the ears.

Although grooming is healthy, some cats practice excessive grooming, causing problems such as skin inflammation, hair

Cats are fastidious about grooming and will spend long, leisurely periods cleaning their coats each day. Using their extremely flexible necks and shoulders, they can reach nearly every part of their body with tongue and teeth.

TERRITORY

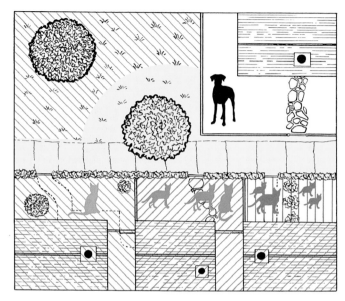

The extent of a cat's territory depends on its position in the hierarchy. Queens with kittens (far right in picture) have small territories which they defend fiercely. A tom (left) will probably have the most extensive area. All cats will avoid gardens with dogs, but some areas, (eg paths), will be communal.

Cats establish territories for much the same reasons that humans build or buy homes—to have a safe place of their own for sleeping, eating, defecating, and playing. Like humans, cats are territorial by nature. Even house cats who never get outside have favorite places within the house for their needs, even if it's only a room or a part of a chair. Where

Cats use scent marks to indicate territorial limits and to leave behind information for other cats about the status, sex and route of the depositor. Tom cats spray their boundaries with pungent urine. More subtle marks are left by rubbing the chin, forehead and tail against doorways, trees and fences; this action deposits scent from the sebaceous glands.

TERRITORIAL MARKING

Cats identify their property and places by scent marking. They employ various glands for this purpose. Scent glands on the head, called temporal glands, are situated above the eyes on each side of the forehead. The perioral glands are along the lips, and both sets of glands are used for marking when the cat rubs its head against a friend or a chosen object—behavior that appears to give the cat extreme pleasure. Some cats, usually full males, mark their territory by urine-spraying on various boundaries. Head rubbing is used for identifying objects rather than as boundary marking. Some stropping behavior is used to scratch at a cat's boundary marker after spray marking.

Ideally a cat's territory will include a high point from which it can keep an eye on what is going on. The dominant tom does not tolerate competition from other cats within his territory.

several cats live in a house, territories may blur, until all residents jointly claim the house and offer mutual defense against any others. If your cat is not confined indoors, it will also have a territory outside the house and a social position to go along with it. Unwittingly humans have made it easy, in some cases, for cats to choose territories. Fences, sidewalks, driveways, gardens, and shrubbery have set up boundaries that can be easily followed if there are a lot of cats in the area. Sometimes humans assist in designating boundaries by chasing other cats away or breaking up fights.

Cats mark their territories by scratching and depositing scents in their urine and feces or from glands on their bodies. Territories can be as large as 100 acres or more for rural cats and as small as a few feet for house or city cats. In households with more than one cat, territories are sometimes time-shared— one cat gets it in the morning, followed by another in the afternoon.

Cats organize themselves into family-type hierarchies in which every cat has a position and follows certain rules. New cats in the neighborhood must fight to be

CAT WATCHING TIP

You may not think your cat has a territory, but all cats do in some form. Follow your cat out into the yard. Make note of where it goes, what it looks at, what it marks, and how it reacts to other creatures in its proximity. Notice where it settles down and what paths it takes to get to where it wants to be. Note if there is also a common ground where it meets up with other cats, and what kind of social standing your cat seems to have as a member of the group. Do this for several days because the cat might not cover all its territory in just one.

accepted and win territory. Males are organized by strength. The toughest tom becomes the head of the "family," with power over the other members in the ranks below him. Occasional changes occur in position when one member is overthrown or neutered. Although tom cats rule the biggest area of territory, they do not get priority in courtship. Land, not sex, is what puts them at the top.

Females are organized by their motherly accomplishments. The queen with the most kittens is top mama. When queens are neutered, they slide down on the social ladder. Females and neutered males possess only small plots and fight harder than big tom cats to retain their little islands. Cats who own large areas are not as possessive because they have so much territory and are unable to spend enough time protecting it all. But when they decide to fight, they usually win.

Amid the private properties there are common grounds for socializing, mating, hunting, or whatever. To reach these places, cats have to follow certain trails so as not to violate other territories or antagonize enemies (like dogs). Some paths are private, but most are common, like human highways.

LOOKING AFTER YOUR CAT

Keeping your cat healthy is mainly a matter of common sense and proper husbandry.

In the first place, the cat needs to have been properly reared as a kitten and should be regularly vaccinated against the most dangerous feline diseases such as panleukopenia, or infectious enteritis, rhinotracheitis and calicivirus, often called cat 'flu, and feline leukemia virus. All cats should be fed a well-balanced diet and receive regular courses of anthelmintics to make sure that they are free from internal parasites. External parasites such as fleas should be controlled by the application of pest powder or sprays when necessary, or by dosing with a product designed to curtail the fleas' breeding cycle. The cat's toilet tray must be maintained in spotless condition at all times, as must its food and water bowls. Given such care, and lots of love and attention, the cat should always remain in good health.

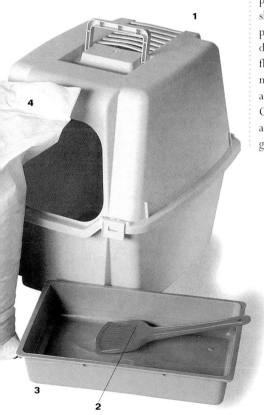

The matter of finding the type of litter and litter container that suits your cat is often a case of trial and error. Shown here are a covered box style container 1, a scoop 2, a basic litter tray 3, and a bag of litter material 4. Dispose of the soiled litter as soon as possible, as cats are reluctant to use a dirty tray. Always wear gloves for this task.

CHOOSING A CAT

The behavior of a domestic cat will be influenced by its gender, particularly if the animal is not neutered. Whereas females will call and slip out of the home in order to find a mate when they are ready to breed, mature tom cats will frequently spray urine around the home as a territorial marker. Neutering is recommended, therefore, not only to prevent unwanted kittens but also to curb this type of undesirable behavior. Some owners claim that female cats are more affectionate and home-loving than males, but after neutering there is really little difference in temperament between them.

The choice between a male or female kitten is of little significance unless you are interested in breeding from your cat. In this case it is a good idea to start out with a female kitten. It is relatively easy to arrange for your cat to be mated with a stud tom in due course, on payment of a suitable fee.

Obviously, if you have been following the show scene by attending such events and reading the specialist press, you will be aware of the top bloodlines that are winning regularly. Your own cat, too, may have already had success on the show bench, but if you hope to improve on her features in the resulting kittens, it is important to make an honest and unprejudiced appraisal of both her strengths and her weaknesses.

If, for example, you notice that her coloration is slightly weak, it is prudent to seek out a sire with very strong coloring. In this way, some of the kittens may show an improvement in their coloration over that of their mother.

Although there can be no guarantees, this approach is most likely to lead to an overall improvement in the quality of your cats.

Choosing can be difficult when confronted with a litter of attractive kittens, such as these Somalis. They are six weeks old, and not yet fully weaned.

Sexing

Sexing kittens is certainly not as easy as it is for adult cats, because their genitals tend to be less pronounced. It is helpful to compare the kittens in a litter if you are in any doubt. Determining their sex becomes fairly straightforward once the young cats are roughly a month old.

A male cat does not have an external penis. Like the female, he has two visible openings below the base of the tail, the upper opening being the anus, but the gap between them is longer than in a female. The penile orifice also tends to be more rounded in shape, whereas the vulval opening in the female resembles a slit. Should you still be in doubt, gentle pressure on each side of the opening in the male should bring the penis into view. A cat's penis is rather unusual, being covered in tiny spines that stick up during mating.

The testes will become evident in male kittens at around four weeks of age as swelling occurs, between the anus and the penile opening. Before this stage, the testes will have descended from the abdomen, where they develop, but will not project into the scrotum.

As a cat matures, it becomes easier, particularly in some breeds, to determine its sex simply by looking at it. Male British shorthairs, for example, develop very distinct swellings on either side of the face, known as jowls, which are not apparent in females. As in the case of many wildcats, they also tend to be slightly larger than females.

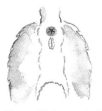

Female kitten. Note proximity of ano-genital openings.

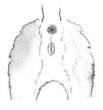

Female cat. Similar in appearance, but a slightly larger space is evident.

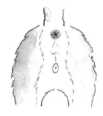

Male kitten. Larger gap than in the female, although testes have not descended.

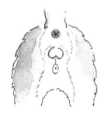

Male cat. Testes clearly visible in the scrotum by this stage.

FEEDING

All cats are active hunters, rather than scavengers. They will take a wide variety of prey, depending on their size and the environment where they are living. The diet of the wildcat varies depending on the types of animals that share its extensive territory, but it is centered mainly on rodents and birds of various types. Larger wild species such as lions and tigers will hunt bigger quarry; tigers pursue large herbivores, such as deer and sometimes even cattle.

Cats are opportunistic, and they will tend to eat whatever they can catch, which may range from small insects to turtles. Fish also form a prominent part of the diet of a number of species. Domestic cats are therefore unusual in readily eating prepared foods. Nevertheless, there are few fussier eaters than cats, and should their food suddenly be changed, they may well starve themselves rather than consume this equally nutritious alternative. Equally, if the food is stale, it is likely to be ignored by the cat.

All cats rely primarily on their sense of smell to determine whether or not to eat a certain food. They will sniff cautiously at it before deciding whether to taste it. In the case of a cat that has been suffering from a respiratory illness, persuading it to eat normally can often prove very difficult, simply because its sense of smell is likely to be impaired.

A sad fact of keeping a cat is that it may catch a bird or rodent. The hunting instincts of domestic cats remain strong, but they can have problems killing their quarry.

Fresh foods

Although many owners now use prepared diet or canned catfoods for their pets, some still prefer to provide them with fresh foods. These should be cooked and allowed to cool down before being offered to the cat. Lungs, liver, and other types of organ meat are frequently used as cat food, but over time they are nutritionally inadequate.

Wild cats eat their entire prey, but the domestic cat fed on organ meat will not have access to the skeleton, which contains most of the body's calcium reserves. As a result, the cat will eventually develop skeletal weaknesses; this is particularly true in the case of kittens, which are growing rapidly. Nor is it only deficiency that can be harmful. Too much liver in a cat's diet will lead to a dietary excess of vitamin A, which can also lead to skeletal abnormalities. This can result in fusion of bones in the shoulders which is painful for the cat.

While fresh foods can be used occasionally, particularly to tempt the appetite of a sick cat, it is very important to mix with these foods a suitable vitamin and mineral supplement, after consultation with your veterinarian, especially if you intend to use this type of diet for your cat for any length of time.

Although there is a popular myth that feeding raw meat to domestic cats can make them aggressive, this is untrue. But there is a possible risk—especially with the high volume of animals processed in modern meat-packing plants—that meat could be contaminated by a range of potentially harmful bacteria, such as *Salmonella*. There is a possibility that your cat could fall ill as a consequence, or might even acquire parasites. Cooking all meat is therefore highly recommended in any event, as a safety precaution. The risk of such infection is much lower in the wild, simply because of the fact that the cat hunts and kills an individual animal and eats it almost at once, thereby eliminating the risk of cross-infection.

Cats may carry or drag their quarry some distance from where it was caught. This is an instinctive attempt to stop other predators from taking it.

Cats will eat the whole animal, in the case of small prey, so that they receive the benefit of the calcium reserves that are contained in the skeleton.

Preparing foods

The ready availability of prepared foods, containing all the essential nutrients required by cats, has been one of the major reasons for cats' burgeoning popularity as pets. The pet food manufacturers have invested huge sums of money to determine the correct formulation for their products, to the extent that there are now so-called "life stage" diets available, catering to the individual needs of kittens and adult and older cats. Even so, standard cat food is still widely used, and should not have any adverse effects on a cat's health.

Canned foods remain the food of choice with most cats, although this type of food is less convenient than the dry foods or semi-moist types and the cans themselves are heavy to carry and bulky to store for the owners. Canned food appears to be favored by many cats because it more closely resembles the cat's natural prey. Canned food has a much higher water content, often as much as 75 percent, compared with dried food which provides a more concentrated source of nutrients.

The feeding preferences of cats are usually quite firmly established early in life, so it is a good idea to offer a range of foodstuffs at this stage. You will then, with luck, have a cat that is less fussy about its food in later life.

Dry foods typically have a water content of just 10 percent. They had a bad press in some countries in the early days, because of links between this type of food and the illness known as feline urological syndrome (FUS). In cats affected by this problem (more males than females), the urine becomes relatively concentrated, and crystals form within the bladder. These then pass down the urethra, which connects the bladder to the outside. The result is not only a painful obstruction but also an impediment to the flow of urine. Rapid veterinary treatment is required to remove the obstruction,

Domestic cats will feed readily on prepared foods, but since they appear to establish their feeding preferences early in life, it can be difficult to get them to change from canned food to a dry diet for example. In many cases cats will starve rather than eat unfamiliar food.

otherwise the cat's condition will deteriorate.

Today, the salt level of dry foods has been increased, to encourage cats fed on this type of diet to drink more fluid, reducing the likelihood of their developing FUS. In addition, the level of magnesium, suspected as the key culprit in the formation of these crystals, has been significantly lowered. In fact, it is now actually lower in dry foods than in many other foods fed to cats, such as sardines.

There are a number of advantages to using dry food. For one thing, the cat's teeth and gums are less likely to accumulate tartar. Dry food is also less likely to attract flies than canned or fresh food—a considerable advantage when the weather is hot. It is also much easier to store, because an opened bag or box does not have to be refrigerated.

This type of food is therefore ideal for "demand" feeding, because it can be left out throughout the day without risk of deterioration, provided that it stays dry. This is ideal for people who are living alone, because you can be sure that your cat will

It is vital to wash the food bowl after each meal, whether you give your cat dry food (1), canned food in jelly (2), or semi-moist food (3). Cats are fastidious about eating freshly presented food. Wash the bowl separately from household plates, rinse, and dry before refilling, especially if you are giving dry food to your pet.

have food available, even if you are late coming home. Unlike dogs, cats rarely overeat when they are provided with free access to food, because their relatively high fat intake, which tends to slow down the emptying of the stomach, means that their appetite is quite rapidly satiated. The other type of prepared food is the semi-moist food, which combines the characteristics of both canned and dry foods. These foods are relatively light and are supplied in envelopes. They have a moister texture than dry foods, as their name suggests. Their water content is typically around 35 percent, and they contain additives to ensure that they do not dry out or turn moldy. Beware: Many semi-moist foods contain a lot of sugar.

GROOMING YOUR CAT

Many cats never really require grooming, but it should nevertheless be a regular part of your relationship. It will give you an opportunity to check your cat's health, and will be welcome if the cat ever needs help with grooming (after it gets into tar or other substances that might be toxic if ingested).

Grooming is best done outside; it keeps the dirt, hair, and fleas out of the house. The next-best places for grooming are the porch, bathroom, or utility room. Indoors, stand the cat on paper or plastic.

Inspect ears, eyes, and claws, cleaning ears with cotton and olive oil and the eye area with cotton and water if necessary. Examine teeth weekly, cleaning to prevent tartar build-up. Examine and trim claws.

Wild longhaired cats molt in spring, but, kept in artificially lit and heated conditions, domestic cats molt all year round, so need daily grooming (two 15–30-minute sessions) or their coats will mat.

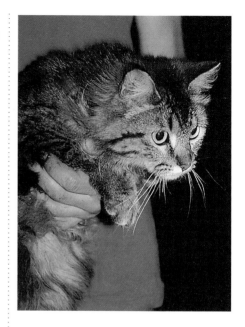

Above: Picked up and supported in the right way, most cats will feel quite secure in human arms.

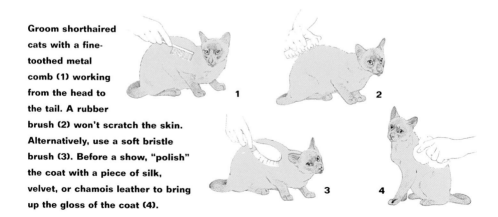

Groom shorthaired cats with a fine-toothed metal comb (1) working from the head to the tail. A rubber brush (2) won't scratch the skin. Alternatively, use a soft bristle brush (3). Before a show, "polish" the coat with a piece of silk, velvet, or chamois leather to bring up the gloss of the coat (4).

Above: Grooming equipment should include a slicker brush (1) for longhaired tails, a wire and bristle brush (2), a wide- and fine-toothed comb (3) for the coat, and a toothbrush (4) for cleaning the face.

Shorthaired cats don't need daily grooming; their coats are easier to manage, and longer tongues make them proficient at self-grooming. Two half-hour sessions a week should be enough.

If there are signs of matted hair, take care of those first with a wide-toothed comb. Other utensils can be used, including a fine-toothed comb to find fleas and a rubber brush to remove dead hair.

For greasy coats, sprinkle in talcum powder or dry cleaner from the pet store, and comb it out quickly. Silk, velvet, or chamois leather cloth will "polish" the coat.

If your cat's coat is very dirty or greasy, you will need to bathe it. Your cat will probably not like water, so give it plenty of love and attention so that the bath doesn't turn into a test of wills. Close all doors and windows to prevent drafts. Place a rubber mat in the tub or basin to prevent slipping.

Fill with 2–4 inches of warm water and use a sprayer to wet the cat. Water should be around body temperature, 101.4°F. Lather with a nontoxic baby or cat shampoo. Rinse thoroughly with warm water.

Wrap in a towel to lift out and dry gently with a towel or hair dryer on low. Avoid drafts until completely dry. Comb gently.

Left: To groom longhaired cats, use a wide-toothed comb (1) to remove debris and tease out mats. Brush some talcum powder or fuller's earth (2) into the coat to add body. Brush out the powder immediately. Use a wire brush (3) to remove dead hair, paying particular attention to the rump. Gently brush the face area with a toothbrush (4) Run a wide-toothed comb through the hair, upward toward the back, and fluff out the ruff. For show cats, use a slicker brush on the tail.

DISORDERS

During a cat's self-grooming, scratching with the hand legs helps dislodge parasites from the fur.

Before your cat comes home with you, it will have to be vaccinated against some of the most widespread and significant viral diseases to which cats are susceptible. Feline distemper, upper respiratory infections, and rabies are included in the vaccinations.

Prior to vaccinations, the cat should be 8–12 weeks old and free of parasites. Vaccinations require annual boosters, which can be given when you take your cat to the veterinarian for its annual checkup.

Cats are also susceptible to a variety of other diseases, disorders, and parasites, some of which also affect humans. Fleas, ticks, mites, lice, and maggots are the major external parasites to look out for during grooming. Some pests transmit diseases.

Internal parasites include a variety of unseen worms and single-celled organisms. The protozoa *Toxoplasma gondaii*, found in cat feces, is particularly significant because it can be transmitted to humans. Pregnant women especially are advised not to handle feces. Regular worming is advised to prevent these problems, which sometimes first manifest themselves as diarrhea.

Just about every part of a cat's body can be affected by some disease: the skin by ringworm, dermatitis, and ulcers; digestion by enteritis, peritonitis, liver and pancreas diseases and obstructions; mouth and teeth by stomatitis; respiratory ailments; eye disorders like conjunctivitis; ear disorders; kidney disease; the circulatory system by anemia, heartworm, and leukemia.

Be especially wary of your cat's health if it vomits, collapses, has diarrhea, has trouble breathing, is bleeding, or has dilated pupils. A loss of appetite is probably not serious unless it lasts for more than 24 hours.

During grooming sessions and daily contact with your pet, you should check for more subtle signs of disease, such as listlessness, sneezing, coughing, cloudy eyes, closed eyelids, mouth odor, pain, constipation, frequent urination, discharges, and change in regular habits.

Cats begin to show signs of old age after 10 years, which translates to about 60 years in a cat's life. (In human terms cats reach age 18 by the end of one year.) The average lifespan for cats is 15 years. Even if they can't live nine lives, they can at least live a long and healthy one if given consistent, responsible care and attention.

CAT IDENTIFIER

The book is divided into five main breeds: Longhaired, Semi-longhaired, Shorthaired, Foreign Shorthaired, and Oriental. These sections are then subdivided into varieties within breeds, such as Peke-faced (Longhaired), and Smoke (Longhaired). Plain, solid-coated varieties are referred to as "self colors," while patterned varieties are referred to as "non-selfs." Each cat is accompanied by a full-color photograph for ease of reference, and at-a-glance symbols, which give tips on care.

Key to Symbols

Grooming **Space**

Each variety of cat is accompanied by symbols which provide you with at-a-glance information on this cat's specific needs and requirements. The two categories—grooming and space—are each divided into four grades. Within the grooming category, for example, one quarter shaded indicates that little grooming is required, while total shading indicates the need for a great deal of grooming.

LONGHAIRED BREEDS

Self-color

Black

One of the oldest of the pedigree breeds, the Black Longhair or Persian is one of the most difficult to produce in top show condition. It is a massive, handsome cat, and the glossy, raven-black coat is complemented by the large glowing eyes.

The black hair is prone to developing rusty tinges, thought to be caused by strong sunlight or damp conditions, and periods of molting cause brownish bars to appear in the flowing coat.

Young black kittens are often quite disappointing, with lots of shading in the undercoat and rustiness in the top coat, but these defects usually disappear with maturity.

Coloring The coat should be dense coal black from roots to tips of hair, free from any tinge or markings or shadings of any kind, and with no white hair. The nose leather is black, and the paw pads black or brown. The eye color is brilliant copper (USA); copper or deep orange (UK), with no green rim.

Build Medium to large and muscular, with large back and shoulders, and a short face.

Temperament Quiet and gentle; not over-demanding.

Blue

The blue color in cats is caused by the action of the dilution factor on black, and some of the earliest Persian imports had this attractive coat color. In the first cat shows, lots of blue cats were exhibited, but they did not closely resemble the cats seen in the show rings today. At the start of the twentieth century, early show faults, such as white lockets and tabby markings, had been largely eliminated, and in 1901 the Blue Persian Society was founded to promote the breeding and exhibiting of these cats. Members of society, including Queen Victoria, owned Blue Persian cats, and this added to their general status and popularity, which remains to this day.

Coloring The blue coat should be one level tone from nose to tail tip, and sound from roots to tips of hair. Any shade of blue is allowed, but in the USA the lighter shades are preferred. The coat must be free from all markings, shadings, or white hairs. The nose leather and paw pads are blue. The eye color is brilliant copper (USA); deep orange or copper without any trace of green (UK).

Build Medium to large and muscular; with large back and shoulders, and a short, round face.

Temperament Quiet and sweet-natured; not over-demanding.

Chocolate

During the breeding and development of the Himalayan or Colorpoint Longhairs, breeders realized it might also be possible to produce self-colored Chocolate and Lilac longhaired cats. This proved quite simple to put into practice, and cats with the desired coat color were bred quite easily, although their body type and coat quality were extremely poor when judged against Persian standards. The pioneer breeders of these varieties also had to contend with the natural fading and bleaching effect on the coat color caused by the chocolate gene, and some of the early cats were very disappointing. Eventually, however, they succeeded in establishing Chocolate Longhair cats of equal quality to their Himalayan cousins. Some North American associations decided to group the self-colored Chocolate Longhairs under the breed name of Kashmir; others grouped them with the Himalayans.

Coloring The color is a rich, warm, chocolate brown, sound from the roots to the tips of the hair, and free from markings, shading, or white hairs. The nose leather and paw pads are brown. The eye color is brilliant copper (USA); deep orange or copper (UK).

Build Medium to large; cobby but elegant, with a short, round face.

Temperament Gentle, affectionate, and generally undemanding.

Cream

In the early days, cream cats were often called "fawns" and were often discarded by keen exhibitors in favor of cats with stronger coat colors. In 1903, Frances Simpson wrote that creams were becoming fashionable, but the first cats of this variety had been considered "freaks or flukes" and were given away. Cream cats were eventually imported into the United States from Britain and soon established themselves as successful show winners. Today's exhibition Cream Persian is a refined and sophisticated breed, exemplifying all the best features of the typical Longhair.

Coloring The requirements for coat color differ between the USA, the UK, and Europe in general. The CFA standard requires one level shade of buff cream, sound to the roots, without markings, and with lighter shades preferred. The GCCF calls for pure and sound pale to medium color, without shadings or markings. The FIFe standard requires pale, pure, pastel cream with no warm tone or any lighter shadings or markings, the color to be sound and even from roots to tips. The nose leather and paw pads are pink. The eye color is brilliant copper (USA); deep copper (UK).

Build Medium to large; cobby but elegant; with a full, round-cheeked face.

Temperament Affectionate and friendly; generally undemanding and sweet-natured.

Lilac

Like the Chocolate Longhair, the Lilac is a fairly new color, created as a by-product of the Colorpoint breeding program. Originally, the breed was difficult to produce with the correct Persian type, but the problem has now been bred out, and the delicate color of the Lilac ensures it has a firm following among cat fanciers. Some North American associations group the Lilac Longhair (with its Chocolate cousin) under the breed name Kashmir; others have grouped them with the Himalayans.

Coloring The color is a rich, warm lavender with a pinkish tone, sound from the roots to the tips of the hair, and free from markings, shading, or white hairs. The nose leather and paw pads are pink. The eye color is brilliant copper (USA); pale orange (UK).

Build Medium to large; rather cobby but elegant, with a round, full-cheeked face.

Temperament Sweet-natured, affectionate and friendly; generally undemanding.

Red

Although this has been a favorite show breed for over a hundred years, in the early days there was some confusion about the true description of the variety's color. Until 1894, shows at London's Crystal Palace offered classes for Brown or Red Tabby Persians, but in 1895 a class for Orange and Cream was added. The Orange, Cream, Fawn, and Tortoiseshell Society revised the standard for the Orange Persian, requiring "the color to be as bright as possible, and either self or markings to be as distinct as can be got." Judges obviously selected their winners irrespective of markings. Over the years breeders selected for either self-colored or tabby in the reds, and by 1912 they had separate classes, still being described as Orange Self or Orange Tabby. The deeper color was selected, and the past 50 years have seen wonderful improvements in Red Persians in the world's show rings.

Coloring The coat should be deep, rich, clear, brilliant red without markings or shadings or ticking. Lips and chin are the same color as the coat. The nose leather and paw pads are brick red. The eye color is brilliant copper (USA); deep copper (UK).
Build Medium to large; cobby and elegant, with a round-cheeked short face.
Temperament Gentle, sweet-natured, and friendly; generally undemanding.

Persian Van Bicolor

This sub-variety of the Bicolor Persian breed may be shown in black and white, blue and white, red and white, or cream and white. However, the color distribution is quite different from that of the Persian Bicolor. The Van Bicolor is basically a white cat with the color confined to the extremities—head, legs, and tail. Only one or two small colored patches on the body are allowed.

Potential pedigree faults include uneven color patches, too little hair, too thin a body, a difference in tail coloration, an elongated muzzle, and ears that are too close together.

Coloring The coat is basically white, with red, black, blue, or cream color on the extremities—head, ears, and tail. The color standards are as for the main Bicolor breed.

Build Medium-sized and rather solid, with a broad, rounded head and short, thick legs.

Temperament Affectionate and friendly; generally undemanding and not over-energetic.

Blue-cream

Blue-cream coloring is the dilute equivalent of tortoiseshell. Just as a tortoiseshell has patches of black and red, so the Blue-cream cat has corresponding dilute patches of blue (from black) and cream (from red). Some early cat fanciers were able to deduce some of the results to be expected by cross-matings between cats of various colors. The biggest problem for early breeders was that they did not recognize the fact that the "marked blue cats," or Blue-creams, were all female, and that the color was sex-linked.

Coloring Requirements for coat color and pattern differ. In North America, the coat is required to be blue with clearly defined patches of solid cream, well broken on both body and extremities. The GCCF requires the coat to consist of pastel shades of blue and cream, softly intermingled. FIFe refers to Blue-cream as Blue Tortie, and the coat requirement is for light blue-gray and pale cream, patched and/or mingled, both colors to be evenly distributed over the body and extremities. The eye color is brilliant copper (USA), deep copper or orange (UK).

Build Medium-sized and well muscled, with a broad chest and round, short head.

Temperament Affectionate, sweet-natured, and generally undemanding.

Cameo

First bred in the USA in 1954, Cameo Persians were the result of matings between Smoke and Tortoiseshell cats of outstanding type. Cameo kittens are born almost white and develop their subtle color as they grow. There are three intensities of coloring within the Cameo group: Shell is very pale, Shaded somewhat darker, and Smoke is darker.

Coloring The white undercoat of the Shell Cameo must be sufficiently tipped with red on the head, back, flanks, and tail to give the characteristic sparkling appearance of the variety. The face and legs may be lightly shaded with tipping. The chin, ear tufts, stomach, and chest are white. Eye rims, nose leather, and paw pads are all rose. The eye color is a brilliant copper.

Build Medium-sized and well muscled, with a wide, round head and short face. The ears are small and neat.

Temperament Naturally affectionate and sweet-natured; generally undemanding.

Red-shaded Cameo

Like the other forms of Cameo, the Red-shaded is a relative newcomer, one of several tipped varieties of Persian and midway between the heavily tipped Smoke and the more lightly tipped Chinchilla. The coat is long, silky, and luxuriant, and the pale, nearly white under-color contrasts with the darker-colored tips, making a most attractively marked cat.

The ears are small, neat, and well set, although ears that are too close are potential pedigree faults. Other potential pedigree faults include too little hair, too thin a body, and a difference in tail coloration. Cameo kittens are born almost white and develop their subtle coloration as they mature.

Coloring The white undercoat has a mantle of black tipping and clearly defined patches of red and light red tipped hairs in the tortoiseshell pattern. This covers the face, down the sides, and the tail, the color ranging from dark on the ridge to white on the chest, stomach, under the tail, and on the chin. The general effect is much darker than the Shell Tortoiseshell. Eye color is a brilliant copper.

Build Medium-sized and well muscled; rather cobby, with a broad chest and a wide, round head with a short face.

Temperament Sweet-natured, affectionate, and generally undemanding.

Chinchilla

Perhaps the most glamorous of the Persians, the Chinchilla has a characteristic sparkling, silvery appearance. The first Chinchilla cats were born by accident when silver tabbies were mated with cats of other colors. Early Chinchillas were much darker than those seen today, but as the breed developed, the lighter cats came to be known as Chinchilla, and the darker ones, when successfully bred to a different standard, were designated the Shaded Silver.

Coloring The cat has a pure white undercoat, sufficiently tipped with black on the head, back, flanks, and tail to give the characteristic sparkling silver appearance of this variety. The legs may be slightly shaded with tipping. The chin, ear tufts, chest, and stomach are pure white, and the rims of the eyes, lips, and nose are outlined with black. The nose leather is brick red, while the paw pads are black. The eye color is green or blue-green.

Build Medium-sized and rather cobby, with a broad, round head.

Temperament Sweet-natured and affectionate; more outgoing than many other longhaired breeds.

Golden Chinchilla

Now recognized as a breed in their own right, Golden Chinchillas are sometimes known as Golden Persians. They are thought to have originated from Silver Chinchillas that carried the red gene, and they were first bred in the United States. Shaded Golden cats are also beginning to appear at shows. These have a rich, warm cream undercoat, with a mantle of seal brown tipping shading from the face, sides, and tail. The legs are the same tone as the face, and the overall effect is of a much darker cat than the Golden form.

Coloring The cat has a rich, warm cream undercoat, sufficiently tipped with seal brown on the head, back, flanks, and tail to give a golden appearance. The legs may be slightly shaded with tipping, and the rims of the eyes, lips, and nose are outlined with seal brown. The nose leather is deep rose; the paw pads are seal brown. The eye color is green or blue-green.

Build Medium-sized and rather cobby, with a broad and round head. The nose is rather snub.

Temperament Sweet-natured and very affectionate.

Peke-faced

Actually a form of the Red Persian, the aptly named Peke-faced is bred to have a face that resembles that of the Pekinese dog: a short snub of a nose, a clear indentation between the eyes, and wrinkles around the eyes. The form is very rare—as, indeed, is the Red Persian from which it springs.

Apart from the face, the Peke-faced has most other Persian traits, including small, rounded, and tufted ears, and thick, silky fur. The compression of the facial features means that these cats often suffer from respiratory and eating difficulties, and their teeth are often overcrowded.

Coloring The color of the long, luxuriant coat should be an even deep red. Because it is impossible entirely to remove the tabby markings from both this and the Red Persian, breeders aim to reduce to a minimum the effect of the tabby gene, although the legs, tail, and face retain traces of the tabby markings. The eyes are a deep copper.

Build Rather solid and cobby, with short, thick legs and large, round paws.

Temperament The rather cross expression belies a sweet-tempered, calm, and affectionate disposition.

Smoke

Black Smoke

The Smoke Persians first appeared in the 1870s, and they were the result of cross-breeding Black, Blue, and Chinchilla Persians. Although the coat appears to be one solid color, the effect is achieved by the very long and very dark tipping on the fur. The pale undercoat is revealed only when the cat moves.

The Black Smoke has a typical silvery frill (ruff) around the neck, which contrasts beautifully with the black head. As with all Smokes, the coat is long, dense, and silky, and requires more grooming than even that of other Persians.

Coloring The undercoat is pure white, deeply tipped with black. In repose, the cat appears black, but in motion the white undercoat is clearly apparent. The mask and points are black, with a narrow band of white at the base of the hairs next to the skin, seen only when the hair is parted. The frill (ruff) and ear tufts are light silver. Nose leather and paw pads are black. The eye color is brilliant copper (USA); orange or copper (UK).

Build Medium-sized and rather cobby, with a broad, round head and snub nose.

Temperament Sweet-natured and affectionate; generally undemanding.

Blue Smoke

The Smoke Persian is often known as "the cat of contrasts," and, although rare, it is an excellent longhair type. The breed has always been popular in the United States. Exhibition Smokes require more than usual attention, because wet weather and excessive sunshine will spoil the appearance of the coat.

The Blue Smoke resembles the Blue Persian, but when it moves, the contrasting white of the undercoat becomes visible. These cats are difficult to breed without tabby markings.

Coloring The white undercoat is deeply tipped with blue so that in repose the cat appears blue, but in motion the white undercoat is clearly apparent. Mask and points are blue with a narrow band of white next to the skin, which is seen only when the hair is parted. The frill (ruff) and ear tufts are all white; the nose leather and paw pads are blue. The eyes are a brilliant copper or orange or copper.

Build Medium-sized and rather cobby, with a broad, round head and snub nose.

Temperament Sweet-natured and affectionate; generally undemanding.

Cream Smoke

The Cream Smoke is a paler version of
the Red Smoke, with the cream
coloring shading delicately on the
sides and flanks until it is almost
white. The Cream Smoke is difficult to
breed without distinct tabby
markings appearing. The long, dense,
silky fur requires frequent and
careful attention if matting is not to
occur. If they are to appear in top
condition, Smokes should be kept out
of both direct sunshine and wet
conditions, but despite this, they are
good mousers in the right
circumstances.

Coloring The white undercoat is deeply
tipped with cream, with clearly defined,
unbrindled patches of darker cream. In
repose, the cat appears to be cream, but in
motion the white undercoat is clearly
apparent. Face and ears are cream,
patterned with a narrow band of white next
to the skin, seen only when the hair is
parted. A blaze of cream tipping on the face
is desirable. The frill (ruff) and ear tufts are
white. The eye color is a brilliant copper.

Build Medium-sized and rather cobby,
with a broad, round head and snub nose.

Temperament Sweet-natured and
affectionate; generally undemanding.

Red Smoke

Although this may, at first glance, appear to be a self-color, the Red Smoke, like other Smoke Persians, has a lighter undercoat, visible when the cat moves. The coat is typically long, dense, and silky.

For breeding purposes, Smokes can be paired, but their features will deteriorate over the generations, unless good Blue or Black longhaired cats are used as out-crosses.

Coloring The undercoat is white, deeply tipped with red. In repose, the cat appears red, but in motion the white undercoat is clearly apparent. Mask and points are red, with a narrow band of white next to the skin, seen only when the hair is parted. The frill (ruff) and ear tufts are white, the eye rims, nose leather, and paw pads are rose. The eye color is brilliant copper.

Build Medium-sized and rather cobby, with a broad, round head and a snub nose.

Temperament Sweet-natured and affectionate; generally undemanding.

Tortoiseshell Smoke

This is a comparative newcomer among Smoke Persians, and females are more likely to be produced than males. They have the characteristic tortoiseshell markings, and the white undercoat is tipped with black. The Tortoiseshell Smoke is available in the standard tortoiseshell colors—red, cream, and black—with a new lilac form (shown here) being developed. Like other Smokes, this is a glamorous and popular breed.

Coloring The white undercoat is deeply tipped with black, with clearly defined, unbrindled patches of red and light red hairs in the pattern of a Tortoiseshell. In repose, the cat appears to be tortoiseshell, but in motion the white undercoat is clearly apparent. The face and ears are tortoiseshell patterned, with a narrow band of white next to the skin, seen only when the hair is parted. A blaze of red or light red tipping on the face is desirable. The frill (ruff) and ear tufts are white. The eyes are a brilliant copper color.

Build Medium-sized and rather cobby, with a broad, round head and a snub nose.

Temperament Sweet-natured and affectionate; generally undemanding.

Tabby

Blue Tabby

Pedigree tabby cats have always caused controversy over their standards of points throughout the cat world. In the early days of the development of breeds, there were arguments about pattern and clarity of markings, and even more disagreement about the correct eye color. Tabby Persians are quite rare in the show rings of the world, possibly because it is difficult to reach the high standard demanded.

Coloring The ground color of pale bluish ivory includes the lips and chin; the markings are very deep blue, affording a good contrast with the gray ground color. A warm fawn patina covers the whole cat. The nose leather is old rose, and the paw pads are rose. The eye color is a brilliant copper.

Build Medium-sized and rather cobby, with a broad, round head and a snub nose.

Temperament Sweet-natured and affectionate; generally undemanding.

Brown Tabby

Although the Brown Tabby is regarded as the original type of the Tabby Persians, the color has lapsed into relative obscurity in recent years. Pedigree Tabby cats have always caused controversy over their standards of points throughout the cat world, and Brown Tabby Persians are no exception. The difficulty of finding suitable out-crosses may have contributed to the problem, and pairing these cats together over several generations results in a loss of type, and it is not easy to produce the desired coloration. The US standard varies from the UK counterpart in permitting both the usual whorls and the so-called "mackerel" patterning of vertical striping on the sides.

Coloring The ground color is brilliant coppery brown; the markings are dense black. The lips and chin are the same color as the rings around the eyes. The backs of the legs should be black from the paw to the heel. Nose leather is brick red, and the paw pads are black or brown. The eyes are copper or hazel (UK).

Build Medium-sized and rather cobby, with a broad, round head and a snub nose.

Temperament Sweet-natured and affectionate; generally undemanding.

Red Tabby

The classic Tabby pattern, sometimes referred to as "marbled" or "blotched," calls for precise, dense markings, clearly defined and broad. A deep red coat with even darker markings are required for the show standard for the Red Tabby Persian, which was originally known as the Orange Tabby.

Although the type of Red Tabby today is generally good, problems over obtaining the correct markings still exist. The pattern can, however, be ascertained in young kittens, and it changes little as the cats mature.

Coloring The ground color is red, including the lips and chin; the markings deep rich red. Nose leather is brick red, and the paw pads are black or brown. The eyes are brilliant copper.

Build Cobby and muscular, with a broad, round head and small, low-set ears.

Temperament Sweet-natured and affectionate; generally undemanding.

Silver Tabby

Silver Tabby Persians are relatively rare these days, largely because of the difficulty of achieving a basically silver coat with black tabby markings. The search for good Silver Tabbies is further complicated by the fact that often the darker kittens in a litter prove to be the best marked adults, whereas those that appeared promising as kittens lose their markings as they mature. The use of Brown Tabbies as out-crosses has given some Silvers brown markings, while Black Persians often lead to Silver Tabbies with orange eyes.

Coloring A ground color of pure pale silver includes the lips and chin; the markings are dense black. Nose leather is brick red, and paw pads are black. The eye color is green or hazel.

Build Cobby and muscular, with a broad, round head and small, low-set ears.

Temperament Sweet-natured and affectionate; generally undemanding.

Tortoiseshell Tabby

The Tortoiseshell Tabby is a cat in which the tabby pattern is the main coat color and this is overlaid with shading or red, while still allowing both tabby and tortoiseshell areas to remain clearly visible. The legs must be evenly barred, with bracelets extending as far as the body marking. The tail, too, must be evenly ringed.

In addition to the Brown Tortoiseshell Tabby shown here, there are Blue and Silver Tortoiseshell Tabbies, both of which have brilliant copper eyes.

Coloring A ground color is a brilliant coppery brown with the lips and chin the same shade as the rings around the eyes; with classic or mackerel markings of dense black and patches of red and/or light red clearly defined on both body and extremities. The eye color is brilliant copper.

Build Cobby and muscular, with a broad, round head and small, low-set ears.

Temperament Sweet-natured and affectionate; generally undemanding.

Tortoiseshell

Popular since the pioneer days of cat breeding, the Tortoiseshell Persian always attracts public interest at shows by its striking coat of black patched with areas of red. The first recorded tortoiseshell cats were shortcoated, but around the early 1900s, longcoated tortoiseshells were seen at cat shows; they have always been popular as pets. Breeders are intrigued by the female-only variety, and enjoy the variety of colors a tortoiseshell queen can produce, depending on the recessive color genes she carries, and on the color and genotype of the male to which she is mated.

Coloring The body color is black and unbrindled and clearly defined patches of red and light red on both the body and extremities. A blaze of red or light red on the face is desirable. The eye color is brilliant copper.

Build Medium-sized, cobby, and broad chested, with a round, broad head and a short nose.

Temperament Sweet-natured and affectionate; generally undemanding.

Calico

These tortoiseshell-and-white cats, once known as Chintz cats in the UK, are referred to as Calico cats in the United States. In the Dilute Calico, the effect of the dilute gene replaces the black color with blue, and the red patches with cream, giving a blue, cream, and white cat. As there are no males in these varieties (very occasionally a male is born, but invariably proves to be sterile at maturity), solid-colored cats are generally used for stud purposes.

Coloring The body color is white with unbrindled patches of black and red; white is predominant on the underparts. The eye color is brilliant copper. The body color of the Dilute Calico is white with unbrindled patches of blue and cream; white is predominant on the underparts. The eye color is brilliant copper.

Build Medium-sized, cobby, and broad chested, with a broad, round head and rather short nose.

Temperament Friendly, sweet-natured and affectionate; generally undemanding.

Colorpoint

Blue Point Colorpoint

The Persian characteristics are dominant in most physical aspects of the Himalayan or Colorpoint—apart from the coloring, of course. The fur is silky, thick, and dense, with an abundant frill (ruff). In Colorpoint kittens, the facial markings or mask are not complete, leaving a typically pale forehead. Deep points are favored in exhibition cats, although the depth of color can never be as intense as in the equivalent Siamese cat.

Coloring The body color is bluish-white, cold in tone, which shades gradually to white on the chest and stomach. The points are blue. The nose leather and paw pads are slate gray. The eye color is deep, vivid blue.

Build Medium-sized, stocky, with a rather solid body and a round, broad face. The large ears are set low.

Temperament Intelligent and playful but gentle and very affectionate; demands a lot of attention.

Cream Point Colorpoint

The character of the Colorpoint combines the best traits of the cats used in its creation—the Siamese and the Persian. It is generally a little livelier and more entertaining than its solid-colored Persian cousins, but less vocal and boisterous than the typical Siamese. The precocious breeding tendencies of its Siamese ancestry have been passed on, with Colorpoint females coming into season and "calling" as early as eight months of age, although the males often do not reach maturity until they are 18 months old.

Coloring The body color is creamy white with no shading. The points are buff cream and should have no apricot tinges. The nose leather and paw pads are flesh pink or salmon coral. The eye color is a stunning deep, vivid blue.

Build Medium-sized, stocky, with a rather solid body and a round, broad face. The large ears are set low.

Temperament Intelligent and playful but gentle and very affectionate; demands a lot of attention.

Red Point Colorpoint

The Red Point Colorpoint is also known as the Flame Point. It is a striking-looking cat, with a body of apricot-toned white and points of a deeper apricot-red. The fur is silky, thick, and dense and, as with all cats in this breed, there is an abundant ruff (frill). Pedigree faults can include crossed eyes, poor bone structure, non-blue eyes, and non-standard markings.

Coloring The body color is creamy white. The points color varies from deep orange flame to deep red. The nose leather and paw pads are flesh colored or coral pink. The eye color is a deep, vivid blue.

Build Medium-sized, stocky, with a rather solid body and a round, broad face. The large ears are set low.

Temperament Intelligent and playful but gentle and very affectionate; demands a lot of attention.

Seal Point Colorpoint

Often mistaken for a longhaired Siamese because its color patterns are similar, the Colorpoint Longhair or Himalayan is a Persian, the product of cross-breeding of Siamese, Birman, and Persian, which first bore fruit in the mid-1930s. The breeding produced the restricted coat patterns and colors usually seen only in Siamese. Available in a wide variety of colors and patterns, the character of the Colorpoint combines the best traits of the cats used in its creation.

Coloring The body color is an even, pale fawn or cream, warm in tone, which shades gradually into lighter color on the chest and stomach. The points are deep seal brown. The nose leather and the paw pads are the same color as the points; the eye color is a deep, vivid blue.

Build Medium-sized, stocky, with a rather solid body and a round, broad face. The large ears are set low.

Temperament Intelligent and playful but gentle and very affectionate; demands a lot of attention.

Blue Tabby Point

All the Tabby Point varieties should have a clearly defined "M" marking on the forehead, spotted whisker pads, and typical "spectacles" marks around the eyes. The tips of the ears and the tail should match.

In addition to the Blue Tabby Point, there are Chocolate, Lilac, and Seal Point Tabbies. The Lilac Tabby Point is exceptionally pretty, with a pure white body color and a clearly lined dark mask.

Coloring The body color is bluish-white, and cold in tone. The mask is clearly lined with dark stripes: vertical lines on the forehead form the classic "M" shape; horizontal lines bar the cheeks; dark spots appear on the whisker pads. The inner ear is light, and there is a "thumb-print" on the back of the outer ear. The legs are evenly barred with bracelets, and the tail is barred. All markings should be broad, dense, and clearly defined. No striping or mottling is allowed on the body, but consideration is given to shading in older cats. The points are light silvery blue, ticked with darker blue tabby markings. The nose leather is blue or brick red, and the paw pads are blue. The eye color is deep, vivid blue.

Build Medium-sized, stocky, with a rather solid body and a round, broad face. The large ears are set low.

Temperament Intelligent and playful but gentle and very affectionate; demands a lot of attention.

Chocolate Tabby Point

All Colorpoint kittens are very inquisitive, friendly, and playful. The markings develop slowly, and the kittens show their true colors a few weeks after birth.

As with other forms of Tabby Colorpoint, the Chocolate form should have a clearly defined "M" on the forehead, spotted whisker pads, and the typical "spectacles" markings around the eyes.

Coloring The body color is ivory. The mask is clearly lined with dark stripes: vertical lines on the forehead form the classic "M" shape; horizontal lines bar the cheeks; dark spots appear on the whisker pads. The inner ear is light, and there is a "thumb-print" on the back of the outer ear. The legs are evenly barred with bracelets, and the tail is barred. All markings should be broad, dense, and clearly defined. No striping or mottling is allowed on the body, but consideration is given to shading in older cats. The points are warm fawn, ticked with milk-chocolate markings. The nose leather and paw pads are cinnamon pink. The eye color is deep, vivid blue.

Build Medium-sized, stocky, with a rather solid body and a round, broad face. The large ears are set low.

Temperament Intelligent and playful but gentle and very affectionate; demands a lot of attention.

Seal Tabby Point

In common with other Colorpoint Persians, the Seal Tabby Points prove very affectionate, and they can become devoted to their owners, often seeking attention. The recognition of the color standards varies slightly between the United States and Britain, but the Seal Point is accepted by both governing bodies, as are the Blue, Chocolate, Red, Lilac, and Tortoiseshell Points. In the United States the Seal Tabby Point is sometimes also known as the Seal Lynxpoint.

In all forms, kittens are born relatively pale in color, with the point markings becoming fully apparent only at the age of about 18 months, and sometimes even later.

Coloring The body color is pale cream to fawn, and warm in tone. The mask is clearly lined with dark stripes: vertical lines on the forehead form the classic "M" shape; horizontal lines bar the cheeks; dark spots appear on the whisker pads. The inner ear is light, and there is a "thumb-print" on the back of the outer ear. The legs are evenly barred. All markings should be broad, dense, and clearly defined. No striping or mottling is allowed on the body, but consideration is given to shading in older cats. The points are beige brown ticked with darker brown tabby markings. The nose leather is seal or brick red; the paw pads are seal brown. The eyes deep blue.

Build Medium-sized, stocky, with a rather solid body and a round, broad face. The large ears are set low.

Temperament Intelligent and playful but gentle and very affectionate; demands a lot of attention.

SEMI-LONGHAIRED BREEDS

American Curl

First seen in California in 1981, the American Curl has only recently been imported into the United Kingdom, and it is not yet recognized by the GCCF.

The original American Curl, Shulamith, was a stray with strangely curled-back ears, and when she produced a litter of kittens, two of these also had ears like their mother. A breeding plan was established, and this breed has, in a comparatively short time, achieved championship status with the Cat Fanciers' Association (CFA) and has attracted a firm and loyal following.

The coat is medium-long and lies flat against the body. The full tail is a notable feature, and the ears should be well furnished with fur.

Coloring All colors and patterns are acceptable.

Build Medium-sized and elegant, with large, round eyes. The distinctive ears should curve back in a smooth arc.

Temperament Friendly, intelligent, playful, and companionable; not over-demanding of constant attention.

Angora

One of the most ancient of cat breeds, originating in Turkey, the Angora was the first of the longhaired cats to reach Europe. In the sixteenth century, they were described as "ash-colored dun and speckled cats, beautiful to behold." The cats were bred from, and some of the kittens went to England, where they were known as French cats. When another type of longcoated cat arrived in Europe from Persia (now Iran), the Angora and the Persian were intermated quite indiscriminately.

The Persian type gradually superseded the Angora type in popularity, and by the twentieth century the Angora breed was virtually unknown outside its native land.

Among the self-colored Angoras are black (shown here), blue, chocolate, lilac, red, cream, cinnamon, caramel, and white.

Coloring The coloring must be dense coal black, sound from the roots to the tips of the hair and free from any tinge of rust on the tips, or a smoke undercoat. Nose leather is black, and paw pads black or brown. The eye color is amber. The jet black coat that is required in this variety is often difficult to produce, particularly in the young cat, for which judges make allowances in show situations.

Build Long, lithe, and elegant, with a tapering, wedge-shaped head.

Temperament Lively, intelligent, and companionable.

Lilac Angora

Precocious as kittens, Angoras are playful and athletic. They are generally affectionate with their owners, but can be aloof with strangers.

Angoras molt excessively in summer, and the loose hair should be combed out daily. The lack of a fluffy undercoat means that the coat does not become matted.

Coloring The long, silky coat, which should have a definite sheen, is a true lilac color—a frosty gray with distinct pinkish overtones. The nose leather and paw pads are black. The eye color is amber.

Build Elegant and lithe, with a well-proportioned body and wedge-shaped head.

Temperament Lively, intelligent, and companionable.

White Angora

During the 1950s and 1960s, North America, Britain, and Sweden imported cats from Turkey to start breeding programs for the development of the Angora breed. In the United States, the Turkish Angora was officially recognized and granted championship status by some associations in the early 1970s, but until 1978, the CFA accepted only the white variety, which is still the most widely recognized form. Eventually, however, a wide range of colors was accepted.

Coloring The coat should be pure white with no other coloring, and the nose leather and paw pads pink. The white coat should be free from any staining, and a smudge of color is permitted in kittens but not in adult cats.

Build Elegant and slender, with a long, wedge-shaped head and large, pointed ears.

Temperament Lively, elegant, and companionable.

Odd-eyed White Angora

Unfortunately, as with other white cats, a significant proportion of these cats is deaf; this handicap can be a serious problem, especially for potential owners living near busy roads. Interestingly, the deafness is usually confined to the blue-eyed side.

Coloring As the White Angora, except that one eye should be blue, and the other green. The large, almond-shaped eyes slant slightly up.

Build Elegant and slender, with a long, wedge-shaped head and large, pointed ears.

Temperament Lively, intelligent, and companionable.

Birman

Blue Point Birman

Also known as the Sacred Cat of Burma, the Birman is quite unrelated to the Burmese, despite the similarity in names. It is a unique breed, for although it bears a superficial resemblance to the Colorpoint Longhair or Himalayan, it has stark white paws on all four feet. Its coat is silky, more like that of the Turkish Angora than the Colorpoint Longhair, and its body type differs from that of the Persian, being longer and less cobby than that breed.

The gloves on the hind paws are called "gauntlets." They cover the entire paw and taper up the back of the leg to a point just below the hock.

Coloring The body is bluish-white, cold in tone, shading gradually to almost white on the stomach and chest. The points are deep blue except for the gloves, which are pure white. The nose leather is slate and the paw pads pink. Eye color should be blue, the deeper and more violet the better.

Build Medium-sized, long, and elegant, with a full-cheeked, round head.

Temperament Intelligent, affectionate, and even-tempered, but less placid than a Persian.

Chocolate Point Birman

The Birman coat is silkier and less dense than that of the Persian. It is comparatively easy to keep well groomed with regular brushing and combing. The white gloves and gauntlets must be kept free from staining by regular washing, careful drying, and the application of a special white grooming powder, which is rubbed in, then completely brushed out, leaving the white areas spotlessly clean.

Coloring The body is ivory with no shading. Points are milk-chocolate of warm tone except for the gloves, which are pure white. The nose leather is cinnamon pink and the paw pads pink. Eye color should be blue, the deeper and more violet the better.

Build Medium-sized, long, and elegant, with a full-cheeked, round head.

Temperament Intelligent, affectionate, and even-tempered, but less placid than a Persian.

Cream Point Birman

The Birman is quieter and more placid than a Siamese, but also less staid than a Persian. It is an inquisitive and affectionate cat, with a rather aloof appearance, giving the impression that it is fully aware of its mystical origins.

Coloring The body is creamy white. The points, except for the gloves, are pastel cream; the gloves are white. The nose leather and paw pads are pink. The eye color is blue.

Build Medium-sized, long, and elegant, with a full-cheeked, round head.

Temperament Intelligent, affectionate, and even-tempered, but less placid than a Persian.

Lilac Point Birman

The Birman matures early; the females can "call" as early as seven months. The queens make excellent caring mothers, and males kept at stud are often renowned for their extra-loving temperament.

Coloring The body has a cold glacial tone, verging on white with no shading. The points are frosty gray with a pinkish tinge, with pure white gloves. The nose leather is lavender pink, the paw pads pink. The eye color is a deep, violet-blue.

Build Medium-sized, long, and elegant, with a full-cheeked, round head.

Temperament Intelligent, affectionate, even-tempered. Less placid than a Persian.

Seal Point Birman

A litter of Birmans normally consists of three, four, or five kittens which are born almost white all over. Within a few days, the points color starts to develop at the edges of the ears and on the tail. The eyes, when they open at seven to ten days, are a cloudy baby-blue which changes to the true blue color as the kittens grow.

Coloring The body is even fawn to pale cream, warm in tone shading to lighter color on the stomach and chest. The points are deep seal brown apart from the gloves, which are pure white. The nose leather should match the points. The paw pads are pink. The eye color is blue, the deeper and more violet the better.

Build Medium-sized, long, and elegant, with a full-cheeked, round head.

Temperament Intelligent, affectionate, and even-tempered, but less placid than a Persian.

Seal Tabby Point Birman

Although purists claim that only Seal Point and Blue Point Birman cats should be considered as the true Sacred Cats of Burma, the CFA in the United States also recognizes the Chocolate Point and Lilac Point varieties, and FIFe in Europe has produced standards of points for both the tabby and red series.

Among the tabby point forms are the Seal Tabby Point (shown here), and the Blue, Chocolate, Lilac, Red, and Cream Tabby Point.

Coloring The body is beige, with dark seal tabby points, except for the gloves which are white. The nose leather is brick red, pink, or seal brown, and the paw pads are pink.

Build Medium-sized, long, and elegant, with a full-cheeked, round head.

Temperament Intelligent, affectionate, and even-tempered, but less placid than a Persian.

Seal Tortoiseshell Point Birman

With the typical long, silky coats and frills (ruffs) around their necks, the tortoiseshell point forms include the Seal Tortoiseshell Point (shown here) and Blue, Lilac, and Chocolate; there are also the same colors in the Tortoiseshell Tabby Forms. Whatever their color, Birmans are alert and interested in whatever is going on. They make excellent pets, and their coats are easier to look after than those of Persian cats.

Coloring The body is beige, shading to fawn. The points, except for the gloves, are seal brown patched or mingled with red and/or light red. The gloves are white. The nose leather is pink and/or seal.

Build Medium-sized, long, and elegant, with a full-cheeked, round head.

Temperament Intelligent, affectionate, and even-tempered, but less placid than a Persian.

Cymric

In the late 1960s breeders of Manx cats in the United States were intrigued to discover that some long-coated kittens occasionally appeared in otherwise normal litters from their Manx queens. Although there were no longhaired cats in any of the pedigrees, it is possible that the recessive gene for causing long hair had been inherited from some of the tailed shorthaired cats used as out-crosses in past generations.

Although the first reaction of the breeders was to let such kittens go as neutered pets, it was decided that the variety could be developed as a separate, very attractive breed in its own right. When choosing a name for the breed, some associations preferred Longhaired Manx, while others accepted Cymric (pronounced koom-rik), the Welsh word for "Welsh." The breed is recognized by some associations and, except for the coat, has the same standard requirements for show purposes as the Manx cat. The coat is of medium length, soft and full, giving a padded, heavy look to the body.

Coloring Accepted in the same colors and patterns as the Manx.
Build Completely tail-less; the hind legs are longer than the front.
Temperament Friendly and intelligent, with a quiet voice.

Maine Coon

One of the oldest natural breeds of North America, the Maine Coon, or Maine Cat, has been known as a true variety for more than a hundred years. As its name implies, it originated in the state of Maine. At one time it was thought that the cat was the product of matings between semi-wild domestic cats and racoons, hence the name "coon," though this is now known to be a biological impossibility.

The brown tabby and white form of the Maine Coon remains the most popular, but the breed is recognized in all colors, and any amount of white is allowed. Both the classic tabby and the mackerel tabby patterns are accepted in any of the following colors: brown, blue, cameo, red, silver, and tortoiseshell.

Coloring The Brown Tabby has a brilliant coppery brown base coat, with dense black markings. In the Brown Mackerel Tabby illustrated here, the markings consist of fine lines running down the body. The backs of the legs, from the paw to the heel, are black. White is allowed around the lips and chin. The nose leather and paw pads are black or brown. The large, slightly oval eyes, are slightly slanted toward the outer base of the ear; although any eye color is permissible, the more brilliant the better.

Build Large and sturdy, with long legs and a long, square-muzzled head.

Temperament Sweet, friendly, and playful; despite the size, amiable and amusing.

Dilute Calico Maine Coon

Considered by their supporters as the perfect domestic pets, typical Maine Coons have extrovert personalities and are very playful and amusing, often teaching themselves tricks. They may take three or four years to develop their full size and stature, being rather slow to mature.

Although the coat is long and flowing, it rarely gets matted, and is easy to care for with occasional combing through.

Coloring The Dilute Calico is also known as the Blue, Cream, and White Maine Coon. There must be white on the bib, belly, and all four paws. White on one third of the body overall is desirable.

Build Large and sturdy, with long legs and a long, square-muzzled head.

Temperament Sweet, friendly, and playful; despite the size, amiable and amusing.

Red Shaded Maine Coon

Any solid or tortoiseshell color is accepted in the Smoke and Shaded groups. The base coat should be as white as possible, with the tips of the hairs shading to the basic color, darkest on the head, back, and paws. The Smoke is densely colored; while the Shaded shows much more of the silver undercoat.

In addition to the Red Shaded Maine Coon, the Silver Shaded form is accepted. Among Smoke varieties are black, blue, cream, and red.

Coloring There is a white undercoat with red tipping shading down the sides, face and tail, with the color ranging from dark on the ridge to white on the chin, chest, stomach, and underside of the tail. Legs are the same tone as the face. Nose leather and paw pads are black.

Build Large and sturdy, with long legs and a long, square-muzzled head.

Temperament Sweet, friendly, and playful; despite the size, amiable and amusing.

Tortoiseshell Maine Coon

The standard for solid colors insists on a coat that is sound to the roots and free from any shading, markings, or hair of another color. Any of the standard colors and patterns are acceptable in this breed, with the exception of Chocolate Point, Lilac Point, and Siamese. Copper, green, and gold eyes are permitted in all varieties, with blue and odd-eyes being acceptable in the White Maine Coon. However, color is a relatively insignificant feature of the breed, and far more emphasis is placed on type.

The coat should be waterproof, heavy, thick, and dense, most prolific around the neck, where it forms a distinctive frill (ruff). Another notable feature is the tail, which should be at least as long as the body from the shoulder blade to the base of the tail. The tail should be wide at the base, tapering to the tip with full, flowing hair.

Coloring The color is black with unbrindled patches of red and light red, with the patches clearly defined and well broken on both the body and extremities. A blaze of red or light red on the face is desirable.

Build Large and sturdy, with long legs and a long, square-muzzled head.

Temperament Sweet, friendly, and playful; despite the size, amiable and amusing.

Norwegian Forest Cat

Known as the *Norsk Skaukatt* in its native Norway, the Norwegian Forest Cat is very similar to the Maine Coon in many ways. It is a uniquely Scandinavian breed whose origins are shrouded in mystery, and it is referred to in Norse myths and mid-nineteenth-century fairy stories.

Having evolved naturally in the cold climate of Norway, it has a heavy, weather-resistant coat. The glossy, medium-length top coat hangs from the spine line, keeping out rain and snow, while the wooly undercoat keeps the body comfortably warm. Its strong legs, paws, and claws make the Forest Cat an extremely good climber in trees and on rocky slopes. It is highly intelligent, nimble, and an excellent hunter.

Coloring All colors except chocolate, cinnamon, lilac, and fawn are accepted, although neither the Colorpoint (Himalayan) pattern nor the Burmese factor is allowed. Type always takes preference over color. There is no relationship between coat and eye color, but clear eye color is desirable.

Build Large, strong, and solidly boned, with a triangular face and long, bushy tail.

Temperament Lively, friendly, and independent; needs access to the garden.

Black Smoke Norwegian Forest Cat

Developed from the indigenous domestic cat, the Norwegian Forest Cat is found in a wide variety of coat colors and patterns. There is no relationship between coat color and eye color, as is expected in most other pedigree breeds.

The long coat of the breed is particularly attractive in the colors that have a silver undercoat, such as the Smoke, Shaded, Tipped, and Cameo series in all colors. In addition to the Black Smoke shown here, there are blue and red forms. Other color types include the Chinchilla, Shaded Silver, Red Shell Cameo, and Red Shaded Cameo.

Coloring There is a white undercoat deeply tipped with black; in repose, the cat appears black; in motion, the white undercoat is clearly apparent. The points and mask are black, with a narrow band of white at the base of the hairs next to the skin. The frill (ruff) and ear tufts are light silver; the nose leather and paw pads are black.

Build Large, strong, and solidly boned, with a triangular face and long, bushy tail.

Temperament Lively, friendly, and independent; needs access to the garden.

Brown Tabby Norwegian Forest Cat

Any of the four tabby patterns is accepted in the Norwegian Forest Cat, and a whole range of colors except the chocolate, cinnamon, fawn, and lilac series is acceptable. Any amount of white on the body is also permitted.

This handsome Brown Tabby is marked with the classic tabby pattern, which shows clearly on the smooth semi-longhaired cat.

Coloring Brilliant coppery-brown base coat with dense black markings. The backs of the legs from paw to heel are black; white is allowed around the lips and chin. Nose leather and paw pads are black or brown.
Build Large, strong, and solidly boned, with a triangular face and long, bushy tail.
Temperament Lively, friendly, and independent; needs access to the garden.

Red and White Norwegian Forest Cat

Even though its features are markedly similar to those of the Maine Coon of the northeastern United States, the Norwegian Forest Cat is a completely separate breed. The likeness is probably more a function of the rugged lifestyles of the ancestors of the two breeds rather than a common bloodline.

Although the amounts of white are not specified for the Norwegian Forest Cat, a cat will look even more striking when, as here, the paws match neatly.

Coloring In bicolor and particolor cats, the solid color combines with white. The color should predominate, with white areas located on the face, chest, belly, legs, and feet. The range of colors is black, blue, red, and cream.

Build Large, strong, and solidly boned, with a triangular face and long, bushy tail.

Temperament Lively, friendly, and independent; needs access to the garden.

Tortoiseshell Norwegian Forest Cat

Strong and hardy, the Norwegian Forest Cat can be very playful while retaining the strongly independent character of its semi-wild ancestors. It enjoys human company and can be very affectionate, but dislikes too much cosseting.

The trouble-free coat periodically needs combing through to keep the undercoat in good condition and to clean the flowing tail and full frill (ruff).

Coloring Black with unbrindled patches of red and light red, the patches clearly defined and well broken on body and extremities. A blaze of red on the face is desirable.

Build Large, strong, and solidly boned, with a triangular face and long, bushy tail.

Temperament Lively, friendly, and independent; needs access to the garden.

White Norwegian Forest Cat

The ideal Norwegian Forest Cat differs from the Maine Coon in having hind legs that are longer than the forelegs, and the standard of points specifies a double coat, which is permitted, but not desirable, in the North American breed.

The Norwegian Forest Cat will be penalized for small size or fine build, for having a round or square head, for small ears, and for short legs or tail. The ears should be wide-based, with lynx-like tufts. The ears are set high, with the outer edges following the lines of the body right down to the chin.

Coloring In the solid colored forms, the coat should be free from any markings, shading, or any color other than the main one. A white cat should have a pure, glistening white coat. The nose leather and paw pads are pink.

Build Large, strong, and solidly boned, with a triangular face and long, bushy tail.

Temperament Lively, friendly, and independent; needs access to the garden.

Ragdoll

The Ragdoll originated in California, and it remains rare outside the United States. The first Ragdoll cats were bred by an American, Ann Baker, whose white longhaired cat, Josephine, was involved in a road accident which left her with permanent injuries. When Josephine eventually had kittens, they were found to have particularly placid temperaments and would completely relax when picked up and cuddled, reminiscent of a rag doll.

The coat is medium long and dense, soft, and silky in texture, lying close to the body, and breaking as the cat moves. The fur is longest around the neck, framing the face, and is short to medium length on the front legs but longer over the body. The tail is bushy.

Coloring The Seal Bicolor (shown here) has a pale fawn or cream body, with deep seal brown points.

Build Long, muscular, and broad-chested, with heavy-boned legs and a large, flat-skulled head.

Temperament Quiet, gentle, and easy-going; generally undemanding.

Bicolor Ragdoll

The Ragdoll is an exceptionally affectionate, loving, and relaxed cat. Although it is generally calm and placid, with a quiet voice, it loves to play and to be petted. The thick coat does not form mats and is therefore quite easy to groom with regular gently brushing of the body and combing through the longer hair on the tail and around the neck.

The body of the Bicolor Ragdoll is light in color; the points—ears, mask, and tail—should be well defined. The mask has an inverted white "V," the stomach is white, and the legs are preferably white. No white is allowed on ears or tail.

Coloring The Seal Bicolor (shown here) has an ivory-colored body; the points are milk chocolate.

Build Long, muscular, and broad-chested, with heavy-boned legs and a large, flat-skulled head.

Temperament Quiet, gentle, and easy-going; generally undemanding.

Colorpoint Ragdoll

The Ragdoll does appear to have an extremely high tolerance to pain, to the point that injuries may go unnoticed. It also has a very mild temperament. These cats are, therefore, best off when living completely indoors, conditions they seem happy to accept.

In addition to the Seal Point shown here, there are Chocolate, Lilac, and Blue Colorpoints. The body of all forms should be light in color, and only slightly shaded, while the points should be clearly defined, matched for color, and in harmony with the overall body color. Even in the lilac form, good contrast between the body and the color of the points is required. The coat itself should be dense, of silky texture, and of medium length. No white hairs are allowed.

Coloring The Seal Point Ragdoll has a pale fawn or cream body with deep seal brown points.

Build Long, muscular, and broad-chested, with heavy-boned legs and a large, flat-skulled head.

Temperament Quiet, gentle, and easy-going; generally undemanding.

Blue Mitted Ragdoll

The body is light in color and only slightly shaded; the points (except the paws and chin) should be clearly defined, matched for color, and in harmony with the body color. The chin must be white, and a white stripe on the nose is preferred; white mittens on the front legs and back paws should be entirely white to the knees and hocks. A white stripe extends from the bib to the underside between the front legs to the base of the tail.

Coloring The body color is cold-toned bluish-white; the points are blue, except for the white areas.

Build Long, muscular, and broad-chested, with heavy-boned legs and a large, flat-skulled head.

Temperament Quiet, gentle, and easy-going; generally undemanding.

Seal Mitted Ragdoll

Temperament Quiet, gentle, and easy-going; generally undemanding.

Mitted Ragdolls may have a narrow white facial blaze in addition to the white on the chin, chest, bib, underbelly, and, of course, the four paws. In addition to the Blue Mitted and Seal Mitted forms, there are also Chocolate and Lilac Mitted Ragdolls.

Coloring The body color is pale fawn or cream; the points are deep seal brown, except for the white areas.
Build Long, muscular, and broad-chested, with heavy-boned legs and a large, flat-skulled head.

Turkish Van

The cat known as the Turkish in Britain and the Turkish Van in Europe and the United States was first introduced to Britain in 1955 by Laura Lushington. Traveling in the Lake Van district of Turkey, she and a friend were enchanted by these cats and eventually acquired the first breeding pair. Turkish Van cats were also introduced independently from Turkey directly to the United States, where they are now recognized by some associations.

The first cats imported from Turkey were inclined to be slightly nervous of human contact, but today's Turkish cats generally have affectionate dispositions. They are strong and hardy, and have a natural liking for water—they will voluntarily swim if given the opportunity and have no objection to being bathed in preparation for show appearances.

The silky coat has no wooly undercoat, making grooming easy.

Coloring Predominantly white, with auburn or cream markings on the face, and a white blaze. The tail is auburn or cream. The eye color is amber, blue, or odd-eyed.
Build Medium-sized and rather heavy, with a short, blunt head.
Temperament Friendly, intelligent, and sociable.

SHORTHAIRED BREEDS

American Shorthair

At the beginning of the twentieth century, a British cat fancier gave a pedigree Red Tabby Shorthair male to a friend in the United States, to be mated with some of the indigenous shorthaired felines. This cat was the first pedigree cat to appear in the records of the Cat Fanciers' Association. Other British cats followed, including a male Silver Tabby, and the register grew with listings of "home-grown" cats as well as imports. At first, the breed was called the Shorthair, then its name was changed to Domestic Shorthair, and in 1966 it was renamed the American Shorthair.

To gain it credence as a natural American breed, registration bodies accepted applications of non-pedigree cats and kittens conforming to the required breed standards, and in 1971 one such cat won the ultimate accolade of the best American Shorthair of the Year in CFA. Despite the influence of the introduction of the British Shorthair imports in the breeding programs, the American Shorthair has retained its distinctive characteristics.

Coloring Accepted in almost any color or pattern. The best-known and most popular variety is undoubtedly the Silver Tabby, but the classic, marbled, or spotted patterns are also highly favored.

Build Medium to large and rather muscular; the head is more elongated, the legs longer, and the ears larger than its British counterpart.

Temperament Good-natured, affectionate, and outgoing; a good hunter.

Tabby

American Blue Tabby

A cat of very even temperament, the American shorthair makes an ideal family pet. It is an intelligent and good-natured animal which gets along well with other breeds and with dogs.

Its short, thick coat is quite easy to keep in good condition with a simple grooming routine. Combing keeps the coat neat, and stroking with the hand or a silk scarf imparts a healthy sheen. The eyes and ears are easily cleaned with a cotton swab, and a scratching post helps the indoor cat to trim its claws.

Coloring The base color of coat for the Blue Tabby, including lips and chin, is pale bluish-ivory with very deep blue markings. The whole coat color has warm fawn overtones. Nose leather is 'old rose' in color; paw pads are rose. The eye color is brilliant gold.

Build Medium to large and rather muscular; the head is more elongated, the legs longer, and the ears larger than its British counterpart.

Temperament Good-natured, affectionate, and outgoing; a good hunter.

111

American Mackerel Tabby

In the Mackerel Tabby, markings should be dense and clearly defined and resemble narrow pencil lines. The legs should be evenly barred with narrow bracelets, and the tail barred. There are several distinct narrow necklaces around the neck. The head is barred, with a distinct "M" on the forehead and unbroken lines running back from the eyes. More lines run back over the head to meet the shoulder markings. Along the spine, the lines run together forming a dark saddle, and fine, pencil-like markings run down each side of the body from the spine.

Coloring The body markings take the form of clear, narrow lines, running down the spine, and with narrow bracelets on the legs.

Build Medium to large and rather muscular; the head is more elongated, the legs longer, and the ears larger than its British counterpart.

Temperament Good-natured, affectionate, and outgoing; a good hunter.

American Silver Tabby

The markings should be dense and clearly defined, the legs evenly barred with bracelets, and the tail evenly ringed. The cat should have several unbroken necklaces on the neck and upper chest. On the head, frown marks form a letter "M," and an unbroken line runs from the outer corner of each eye. There are swirl markings on the cheeks, and vertical lines run over the back of the head to the shoulder markings, which resemble a butterfly. The back is marked with a spine line and a parallel line on each side, with all three lines separated by stripes of the coat's ground color. A large solid blotch on each side of the body should be encircled by one or more unbroken rings, and the side markings should be the same on both sides of the body. A double row of "vest" buttons should run down the chest and under the stomach.

Coloring The base color, including lips and chin, is pale clear silver with dense black markings. Nose leather is brick red, and paw pads are black. The eye color may be green or hazel.

Build Medium to large and rather muscular; the head is more elongated, the legs longer, and the ears larger than its British counterpart.

Temperament Good-natured, affectionate, and outgoing; a good hunter.

Tortoiseshell

American Blue Tortoiseshell

In exhibition, American Shorthairs may be penalized for excessive cobbiness or ranginess in conformation. Points will also be deducted for obesity or boniness. The tail should not be too short, but should be heavy at the base and taper to an apparently blunt end.

Coloring Base color of coat, including lips and chin, is pale bluish-ivory, with classic or mackerel markings of very deep blue and patches of cream clearly defined on both body and extremities. A blaze of cream on the face is desirable, and warm fawn overtones suffuse the whole body. The eye color is brilliant gold or hazel.

Build Medium to large and rather muscular; the head is more elongated, the legs longer, and the ears larger than its British counterpart.

Temperament Good-natured, affectionate, and out-going; a good hunter.

American Brown Tortoiseshell

As befits a cat that originated in the outdoors, the American Shorthair has thick, dense fur and is athletic and strong. The breed will show affection to the entire family, but it is a bold and inquisitive cat, which needs the freedom to roam.

Coloring The base color of coat is brilliant coppery brown with classic or mackerel markings of dense black and patches of red and/or light red clearly defined on both body and extremities; a blaze of red or light red on the face is desirable. Lips and chin should be the same shade as the rings around the eyes. The eye color is brilliant gold.

Build Medium to large and rather muscular; the head is more elongated, the legs longer, and the ears larger than its British counterpart.

Temperament Good-natured, affectionate, and outgoing; a good hunter.

American Wirehair

The first wirehaired cat was a red and white male named Adam. He was first mated to his normal-coated littermate, and then to other, unrelated shorthaired cats, and from these beginnings a new breed was born. All American Wirehair cats are descended from Adam, and breeding stock has been very carefully selected over the years to guarantee refinement and viability.

Owners say that the Wirehair rules the home and other breeds with an "iron paw" but makes a devoted parent. The unusual wiry coat is easy to maintain in peak condition by correct feeding. These cats need minimum grooming.

Coloring All colors and patterns are accepted.

Build Medium-sized and well-muscled, with a round head, well-developed muzzle, and large, round eyes.

Temperament Affectionate, inquisitive, and playful; a strongly independent character.

British Shorthair

The breed probably evolved from domestic cats introduced to the British Isles by the Roman colonists some 2,000 years ago. However, today's pedigree Shorthairs must conform to strict standards of points and differ quite considerably from the common domestic or farm cat.

Shorthairs appeared in substantial numbers in the first cat shows held toward the end of the nineteenth century, then seemed to lose their popularity in favor of the Persian and Angora cats which were specially imported for the show scene.

It was not until the 1930s that a general resurgence of the breed began, and selective breeding produced cats of good type and the desired range of colors. In the early days, solid colors were preferred to the patterned varieties, the most highly prized of all being the blue-gray, sometimes given solitary breed status as the British Blue.

British Shorthairs suffered a setback during World War II, when many owners had to give up breeding pedigree kittens and neutered their cats. In the post-war years, very few pedigree stud males remained, and the Shorthair's type suffered after out-crosses were made with short-haired cats of Foreign type. Matters were redressed during the early 1950s.

Coloring Accepted in almost any color or pattern. The most popular of the British Shorthairs is the self-colored British Blue (shown here), but tabby and tortoiseshell varieties are also highly favored.

Build Large and rather muscular; the head is very broad, the legs are short to medium length, and ears are set far apart.

Temperament Gentle and undemanding; generally calm and affectionate.

Self-color

British Black

Often considered the "native" British cat, the Black is just one of the many colors and patterns within this group. It is thought that the first shorthaired cats were brought to Britain with the invading Romans and that the British Shorthair is descended from these cats.

Although it has a short coat, this is quite dense and needs regular grooming by brushing and combing right through to the roots every day. It is particularly important to accustom all kittens to this daily procedure from a very early age so that it is not resented later. The eyes and ears should be gently cleaned with a cotton swab whenever necessary, and the coat may be polished with a grooming mitt or a silk scarf.

Coloring The Black is one of the oldest varieties known, and it is often mismarked with a white locket. In a show cat, no white hairs are allowed at all. The true Black Shorthair must have a shining coat, jet black to the roots and with no rusty tinge. The nose leather is black, and the paw pads are black or brown. The eye color is gold, orange, or copper with no trace of green.

Build Solid and cobby, with a rather heavy feel; the head is large and round with small, neat ears.

Temperament Sweet-natured, calm, and gentle; an excellent pet and generally undemanding.

British Blue

The British Blue is one of the most popular and one of the longest-established varieties in this group. Like all British Shorthairs, the Blue has a sweet, gentle nature and makes an undemanding, quiet-voiced pet.

Coloring The coat should be very even in color and of a light to medium blue tone, lighter shades being preferred. No tabby or white markings are allowed anywhere. Nose leather and paw pads are blue. The eye color is gold, orange, or copper.

Build Solid and cobby, with a rather heavy feel; the head is large and round with small, neat ears.

Temperament Sweet-natured, calm, and gentle; an excellent pet and generally undemanding.

British Chocolate

This is a relatively new color in this breed. Like the Lilac Shorthair, it is a by-product of the colorpoint breeding program. British Chocolates are often used as out-crosses for colorpoint breeding, because they commonly carry the gene for the restricted coat pattern.

Coloring The short, plush coat should be an even, rich, dark brown, solid to the roots, with no shading or markings. Eye color is yellow, orange, or copper.

Build Solid and cobby, with a rather heavy feel; the head is large and round with small, neat ears.

Temperament Sweet-natured, calm, and gentle; an excellent pet and generally undemanding.

British Cream

The Cream Shorthair is one of the more difficult colors to breed successfully. Early Creams were prone to undesirable tabby markings, but selective breeding has largely minimized the fault, which is, in any case, more obvious in summer, when the coat is shorter.

Coloring The Cream Shorthair should have no tabby markings in the rich, light cream coat. There must be no white markings anywhere, and the cream color should be sound to the roots. The nose leather and paw pads are pink. The eye color is gold, orange, or copper.

Build Solid and cobby, with a rather heavy feel; the head is large and round with small, neat ears.

Temperament Sweet-natured, calm, and gentle; an excellent pet and generally undemanding.

British Lilac

Another of the newer colors that has resulted from the Colorpoint breeding program, the Lilac has an attractive pinky gray coat. Like other British Shorthairs, the Lilac has a sweet and gentle nature. It is generally calm and intelligent, and readily responds to affection.

Coloring The short, plush fur is an even, solid, frosty gray with a pink tinge. The eye color is orange or copper.

Build Solid and cobby, with a rather heavy feel; the head is large and round with small, neat ears.

Temperament Sweet-natured, calm, and gentle; an excellent pet and generally undemanding.

British White

Like the White Persian, the British White comes in three different varieties, Orange-eyed, Blue-eyed (shown here), and Odd-eyed, each with its own breed designation. Adults of the breed have a pure, brilliant white coat, but kittens may show some pale markings on the head, and these can be a useful indication of the cat's genotype. A blue-based White kitten, for example, may show pale blue marking, while a black-based kitten may show black markings—this is one of the few breeds that sometimes shows its genes on its forehead.

As with all British Shorthairs, the tail length should be in proportion to the body, and it should be thick at the base, tapering to a rounded tip.

Coloring The White Shorthair of good show type is one of the most striking of British Shorthairs. The coat must be pure white with no sign of yellow tingeing; the nose leather and paw pads are pink. The Blue-eyed White has eyes of a deep sapphire blue and is penalized in the show ring for green rims or flecks in the eye. The Orange-eyed White has deep orange, gold, or copper eye color. The Odd-eyed White has one orange eye and one blue eye.

Build Solid and cobby, with a rather heavy feel; the head is large and round with small, neat ears.

Temperament Sweet-natured, calm, and gentle; an excellent pet and generally undemanding.

Non-self-color

British Blue and White Bicolor

Bicolor Shorthairs are cats of just two colors—a standard color with white. It is important that the markings are distributed as symmetrically as possible to present a balanced impression.

The cats may be black and white, blue and white (as shown), red and white, or cream and white, and there must be no tabby markings in the self-colored areas. The markings that make up the self-color portions should start immediately behind the shoulders around the barrel of the body and include the tail and hind legs, leaving the hind paws white.

Coloring Symmetry of coloring is desirable, with not more than half the cat white. The self-color should be a good shade of medium blue. The ears and mask should be self-color, with the shoulder, neck, forelegs and feet, chin, lips, and blaze white. The nose leather and paw pads are usually pink. The eye color is gold, orange, or copper.

Build Solid and cobby, with a rather heavy feel; the head is large and round with small, neat ears.

Temperament Sweet-natured, calm, and gentle; an excellent pet and generally undemanding.

British Cream and White Bicolor

Unlike their Persian counterparts, the British Bicolor has always been a popular breed, partly, no doubt, because their character makes them an excellent family pet—affectionate, intelligent, and sociable. In addition, they are easy to groom and have no special dietary requirements.

In exhibition, the Bicolor will be penalized for brindling or tabby markings, and is likely to be disqualified if white areas predominate.

Coloring Symmetry of coloring is desirable, with not more than half the cat white. The ears and mask should be self-color, with the shoulder, neck, forelegs and feet, chin, lips, and blaze white. The nose leather and paw pads are usually pink. The eye color is gold, orange, or copper.

Build Solid and cobby, with a rather heavy feel; the head is large and round with small, neat ears.

Temperament Sweet-natured, calm, and gentle; an excellent pet and generally undemanding.

British Blue-cream

This dilute variety of the Tortoiseshell is a female-only variety, bred from crosses between British Blues and Creams, Creams and Tortoiseshells, or Blues and Tortoiseshells. This cat nevertheless shares all the normal characteristics of the average British Shorthair, including all typical short, dense fur and rather short, tapered tail.

Coloring In the UK the standard calls for the coat to be softly intermingled with the two shades, but in the United States the variety is required to have a distinctly blue coat with cream patches. Nose leather and paw pads are blue and/or pink. The eye color should be gold, orange, or copper.

Build Solid and cobby, with a rather heavy feel; the head is large and round with small, neat ears.

Temperament Sweet-natured, calm, and gentle; an excellent pet and generally undemanding.

British Calico

Often called the Tortoiseshell-and-white, the Calico is very difficult to breed to top exhibition standard. It should be equally balanced in black and red, both light and dark on white.

This variety is penalized for brindling, tabby markings, unbroken color on the paws, and unequal markings, and it is disqualified if the white areas predominate.

Coloring The colors must be brilliant, and the cat must have no sign of brindling or tabby markings. The patching should cover the top of the head, the ears and cheeks, the back and tail, and parts of the flanks. There should be a white blaze down the face. The nose leather and paws are pink and/or black, and the eye color is gold, orange, or copper (hazel is also allowed by some associations).

Build Solid and cobby, with a rather heavy feel; the head is large and round with small, neat ears.

Temperament Sweet-natured, calm, and gentle; an excellent pet and generally undemanding.

British Colorpoint

In the 1970s, a structured breeding program was devised to produce a cat of British Shorthair type but with the restricted Colorpoint or Himalayan coat pattern of the Siamese. This factor was introduced by matings to Colorpoint Longhairs, as their type was much closer to that of the British than the longer-faced Siamese.

Coloring All the usual Colorpoint colors are available, including seal, blue, chocolate, lilac, red, and cream, as well as the associated colors of the tabby and tortoiseshell-tabby. The color of the Lilac Tortoiseshell Colorpoint (shown here) is almost ethereal, with the points being delicately mingled shades of palest lilac and delicate cream. Although the standard of points requires eye color in the Colorpoint to be a clear, definite blue, this has proved difficult to achieve.

Build Solid and cobby, with a rather heavy feel; the head is large and round with small, neat ears.

Temperament Sweet-natured, calm, and gentle; an excellent pet and generally undemanding.

British Smoke

Smoke-patterned cats are of standard feline colors, but instead of the color being sound to the roots, the undercoat is white or silver. In repose the cat at first appears to be self-colored, but in motion, the white or silver undercoat is apparent, giving a shot-silk appearance. In each sub-variety, the nose leather, paw pads, and eye color required is the same as for that of the relevant self-color. British Shorthair Smoke cats are bred in a variety of colors, but the various associations each have a limited range of those that are officially recognized.

Coloring In the Black Smoke (shown here), the white or silver undercoat is deeply tipped with black. In repose the cat appears black; in motion the pale undercoat is clearly apparent. The nose leather and paw pads are both black. The eye color may be either gold or copper. In the Blue Smoke, the undercoat is white or silver, deeply tipped with blue. The cat in repose appears blue but, as with the black, in motion the pale undercoat is clearly apparent. Nose leather and paw pads are blue. The eye color may be gold or copper.

Build Solid and cobby, with a rather heavy feel; the head is large and round with small, neat ears.

Temperament Sweet-natured, calm, and gentle; an excellent pet and generally undemanding.

British Spotted

Another separately classified tabby pattern and often regarded as the most glamorous, the British Spotted has a pattern that is similar to that of wild cats, and it has always been highly sought after.

The spots can be round, oval, oblong, or rosette-shaped. The head markings should be the same as those required for the classic tabby. The legs should be clearly spotted, and the tail spotted or with broken rings. Spotted cats are penalized when the spots are not distinct, and for having bars, except on the head.

Coloring In the Silver Spotted (shown here), the dense black markings are on a background of very pale, silvery hair. In the Blue Spotted, the pattern consists of blue-gray spots on a lighter background, with enough difference in color to afford a good contrast between the markings and base coat. The standard requires that the spots are as numerous and as clearly defined as possible, with spots or broken rings on the tail. The presence of white in the coat is regarded as a fault. Eye color should correspond to coat color.

Build Solid and cobby, with a rather heavy feel; the head is large and round with small, neat ears.

Temperament Sweet-natured, calm, and gentle; an excellent pet and generally undemanding.

British Tabby

The markings should be dense and clearly defined, the legs evenly barred with bracelets, and the tail evenly ringed. The cat should have several unbroken necklaces on the neck and upper chest. On the head, frown marks form a letter "M," and an unbroken line runs back from the outer corner of each eye. There are swirl markings on the cheeks, and vertical lines run over the back of the head to the shoulder markings. The back is marked with a spine line and a parallel line on each side. A large solid blotch on each side of the body should be encircled by one or more unbroken rings, and the side markings should be the same on both sides of the body.

Coloring A wide range of colors is found, although associations around the world differ considerably in their rules. Varieties are penalized for incorrect eye color, white anywhere, and incorrect markings.

Build Solid and cobby, with a rather heavy feel; the head is large and round with small, neat ears.

Temperament Sweet-natured, calm, and gentle; an excellent pet and generally undemanding.

British Blue Tabby

Like other British Tabbies, there are three acceptable patterns—the classic, the mackerel, and the spotted. In dilute varieties, like the Blue Tabby, the pattern is more diffuse.

Temperament Sweet-natured, calm, and gentle; an excellent pet and generally undemanding.

Coloring Ground color, including lips and chin, should be pale bluish-ivory, with very deep blue markings, affording good contrast with the ground color. There should be an overall warm fawn patina. Nose leather is old rose; paw pads rose. Eye color is gold or copper.

Build Solid and cobby, with a rather heavy feel; the head is large and round with small, neat ears.

British Red Tabby

The Red Tabby shown here has the typical classic pattern on a slightly lighter red base. The desired unbroken "necklaces" can be seen quite clearly around the cat's neck. As with all British Shorthairs, the Red Tabby has relatively short legs and a powerful, rather muscular body.

Build Solid and cobby, with a rather heavy feel; the head is large and round with small, neat ears.

Temperament Sweet-natured, calm, and gentle; an excellent pet and generally undemanding.

Coloring Ground color is red, including lips and chin. Markings are a deep, rich red, quite distinct from the ground color. Nose leather and paw pads are brick red. Eye color is gold, orange, or copper. (Some associations also accept hazel eye color.)

British Red Mackerel Tabby

In the Mackerel Tabby, markings should be dense, clearly defined, and resemble narrow lines. The legs should be evenly barred with narrow bracelets, and the tail barred. There are several distinct narrow necklaces around the neck. The head is barred, with a distinct "M" on the forehead, and unbroken lines running back from the eyes. More lines run back over the head to meet the shoulder markings. Along the spine the lines run together forming a dark saddle, and fine, pencil-like markings run down each side of the body from the spine.

Coloring Lines run down from the spine, but the markings are the same as for the other Tabbies.

Build Solid and cobby, with a rather heavy feel; the head is large and round with small, neat ears.

Temperament Sweet-natured, calm, and gentle; an excellent pet and generally undemanding.

British Silver Tabby

The Silver Tabby's coat pattern shows up extremely well in black on pale silver. The necklaces and eye lines should be clearly defined. All Tabbies have affectionate natures and make good pets, but the Silver Tabby is considered especially friendly.

Coloring Ground color is a pale clear silver, including lips and chin, and markings are dense and black. Nose leather is brick red; paw pads are black. Eye color may be green or hazel.

Build Solid and cobby, with a rather heavy feel; the head is large and round with small, neat ears.

Temperament Sweet-natured, calm, and gentle; an excellent pet and generally undemanding.

British Tipped

A relatively recent development, the Tipped was produced by introducing the Chinchilla into the British breeding program. The result is a shorthaired cat of the British type, but with the tipped, sparkling coat so typical of the Chinchilla.

Coloring A genetically silver variety, the color is restricted to the very tips of the hairs of the coat, while the undercoat is so pale that it appears to be white. The eyes are deep orange or copper, except in the Black-tipped (shown here), when they are green.

Build Solid and cobby, with a rather heavy feel; the head is large and round with small, neat ears.

Temperament Sweet-natured, calm, and gentle; an excellent pet and generally undemanding.

British Tortoiseshell

A mixture of different colors makes for a most appealing cat, with the added distinction that no two Torties are ever alike. As with all Tortie breeds, this is usually a female-only variety, and it is bred in a wide range of colors.

Coloring Black and red markings, both dark and light, should be equally balanced over the cat's head, body, legs, and tail. Colors should be brilliant, free from blurring, brindling, and tabby patches, and with no white markings. A red blaze down the face is desired. The nose leather and paw pads should be pink and/or black. Eye color is gold, orange, or copper (hazel is also allowed by some associations).

This variety is penalized for brindling, tabby markings, unequal balance of color, and unbroken color on the paws, and is disqualified for any white markings.

Build Solid and cobby, with a rather heavy feel; the head is large and round with small, neat ears.

Temperament Sweet-natured, calm, and gentle; an excellent pet and generally undemanding.

Chartreux

Native to France, the Chartreux is said to have been bred exclusively by Carthusian monks as long ago as the sixteenth century. The monks lived in the monastery near the town of Grenoble, world-famous for its unique liqueur, known as Chartreuse. The naturalist Georges Louis Buffon's work *Histoire Naturelle*, published in 1756, records details of the self-blue feline, and in the 1930s a French veterinarian suggested that the breed should have its own scientific name, *Felis catus cartusianorum*.

Today's Chartreux should not be confused with the British Blue or the European Shorthaired Blue. It is massively built, with a very distinctive jowled head, more pronounced in the male than in the female, and is a blue-only breed.

The dense coat needs regular combing to keep the wooly undercoat in good condition, and brushing enhances the way in which the coat stands away from the body—a breed characteristic.

Coloring Any shade of blue, from pale blue-gray to deep blue-gray; paler shades are preferred and uniform tone is essential. Eye color is vivid deep yellow to deep copper.

Build Medium to large, firm and muscular, with a strong head and skull that is broad.

Temperament Self-assured and affectionate; will live happily confined in a house.

European Shorthair

This show breed has been naturally developed from the indigenous cat of continental Europe. Its standard of points is similar to that of the British Shorthair, and it is presumed to be totally free of any admixture of other breeds. The first European Shorthairs were descended from cats introduced to Northern Europe by invading armies of Roman soldiers, who brought their cats with them in order to keep down vermin in their food storage areas.

The short dense coat is easy to maintain with a few minutes daily combing to keep the undercoat in good condition. The eyes and ears should be cleaned regularly with a slightly moistened cotton swab.

Coloring All colors and patterns are accepted, including classic (shown here), mackerel, and spotted tabby. All markings must be clearly defined on a paler background.

Build Medium-sized, with a fairly large, round head and widely set, round eyes.

Temperament Placid and good natured; an ideal family cat.

European Black Spotted Shorthair

Many European Shorthairs have British Shorthair ancestors and are found in a similar range of coat colors and patterns. Tabbies in the silver range are especially popular, although reds, creams, and blue-creams are also found. The European Black Spotted Shorthair is the black version of the Silver Spotted. It has the clearly defined marks on the flanks, but with the pattern tending to form mackerel strips over the ribs.

Coloring In the silver tabby group, the markings are of the main varietal color etched on a base color of pure pale silver. There should be no ticked hairs or brindling in the pattern. The three tabby patterns—classic, mackerel, and spotted—are accepted, and the six accepted varieties are Black Silver Tabby, Blue Silver Tabby, Red Silver Tabby, Cream Silver Tabby, Black Torbie Silver Tabby, and Blue Torbie Silver Tabby. Eye color may be green, yellow, or orange, but green is preferred.

Build Medium-sized, with a fairly large, round head and widely set, round eyes.

Temperament Placid and good natured; an ideal family cat.

European Mackerel Tabby Shorthair

The European Shorthair gave us the word "tabby" in a round-about way. Weavers in Iraq duplicated the colors and patterns of the cat's coat in the silks they exported to Europe, dubbing the fabrics with the name.

The European Shorthair is a territorial cat, and can be combative toward other cats invading its territory. However, it is affectionate toward its owners, females in particular becoming attached to their particular family.

All European Shorthairs will breed prolifically if given the opportunity, producing much larger litters than many other breeds. They are also long-lived cats.

Coloring The non-silver tabby group may have a coat pattern blotched (in the classic tabby style), mackerel, or spotted. The six accepted varieties are Black Tabby, Blue Tabby, Red Tabby (shown here in a mackerel pattern), Cream Tabby, Black Tortoiseshell Tabby, and Blue Tortoiseshell Tabby. All may have green, yellow, or orange eye color.

Build Medium-sized, with a fairly large, round head and widely set, round eyes.

Temperament Placid and good natured; an ideal family cat.

Exotic Shorthair

In the development of British and American Shorthairs, and during the introduction of alternative color factors in the Persians, breeders occasionally mated together pedigree cats of longhaired and shorthaired varieties. This was generally done as a single exercise, the offspring being back-crossed to the main breed in successive generations to strengthen the desired traits.

During the 1960s, cats of mixed Shorthair and Persian lineage were, with the approval of the board of the CFA, given the breed name Exotic Shorthair. The breed is, in essence, a shortcoated version of the typical Persian, with the conformation of the latter, but the added bonus of a coat that is relatively easy to care for. The coat stands out from the body and is longer than that of the British or American Shorthair cat breeds.

Coloring The self-colored Cream Exotic Shorthair (shown here) should be an even shade of buff-cream throughout with no shading or markings; the lighter shades are preferred. The nose leather and paw pads are pink. The eye color is brilliant copper.
Build Medium-sized and cobby, with a large, round head and small, low-set ears.
Temperament Sweet-natured and affectionate; generally undemanding.

137

Exotic Bicolor

Bicolored Exotic cats should have clear and well-distributed patches of color. The face should be patched with color and with white.

In addition to the bicolors seen in the American Shorthair, there are three "Van" color forms. The coat of the Van Bicolor is white with unbrindled patches of black, blue, red, or cream confined to the head, tail, and legs, although one or two small colored patches on the body are allowed. The coat of the Van Tricolor is white with unbrindled patches of both black and red confined to the head, tail, and legs, although up to three small colored patches on the body are allowed.

The coat of the Van Blue-cream-and-white is white with unbrindled patches of both blue and cream confined to the head, tail, and legs, although one or two small colored patches on the body are allowed.

Coloring The coat of the Bicolor is white with unbrindled patches of black, blue (shown here), red, or cream, as seen in the American Shorthair. Nose leather and paw pad color corresponds with the basic coat color. The eye color is brilliant copper.

Build Medium-sized and cobby, with a large, round head and small, low-set ears.

Temperament Sweet-natured and affectionate; generally undemanding.

Exotic Blue

In temperament the Exotic Shorthair is quiet, gentle, and placid. It is an ideal show cat, easy to prepare for the show ring, and enjoys being handled and admired.

The medium-length coat is quite easy to comb through, and being groomed from the tail toward the head encourages the plush fur to stand away from the body. Body condition and shining fur is achieved by correct feeding, and the eyes and ears are kept immaculate by gentle cleaning with a cotton swab.

Coloring An even tone of blue stretches from the nose to the tip of the tail, and is sound to the roots; lighter shades are preferred. Nose leather and paw pads are blue, and the eye color is brilliant copper.

Build Medium-sized and cobby, with a large, round head and small, low-set ears.

Temperament Sweet-natured and affectionate; generally undemanding.

Exotic Calico

The Exotic Shorthair is the ideal breed for the owner who craves for a cat with true Persian type, but does not have the time necessary to care correctly for the demanding long Persian coat. Exotics are indeed a shortcoated version of their Persian ancestors, and show standards for the two breeds, apart from the coat, are almost identical.

Coloring The coat is white with unbrindled patches of black and red, with white predominant on the underparts. Eye color is brilliant copper. The Dilute Calico Exotic (shown here), also known as the Blue Tortie and White, has well-distributed patches of light to medium blue, pale cream, and white.

Build Medium-sized and cobby, with a large, round head and small, low-set ears.

Temperament Sweet-natured and affectionate; generally undemanding.

Exotic Colorpoint

Another descendant of the American Shorthair, the Exotic Shorthair was developed through selective breeding of the American Shorthair with the Longhair or Persian breeds. The Exotic Colorpoint exhibits the Himalayan effect, with a pale body and color on the points—face, tail, legs, and paws. The cat illustrated is a Blue Tabby Colorpoint.

Coloring The six main colors are accepted—seal, blue, chocolate, lilac, red, and cream; the associated colors of tortoiseshell, tabby, and tortoiseshell-tabby are also accepted. There must be good contrast between the body and points color; the points should be free from white hairs, and the body ideally free from shading, which, if present, should tone with the points. Nose leather and paw pads correspond with the individual points' color. Eye color must be clear blue.

Build Medium-sized and cobby, with a large, round head and small, low-set ears.

Temperament Sweet-natured and affectionate; generally undemanding.

Exotic Shaded Silver

The coat of all Exotic Shorthairs is a prominent feature. It should be medium in length, yet plush and soft. It must not lie flat to the body nor appear to flow, being intermediate in nature. Exotic Shorthairs make ideal pets, possessing the characteristics of both main ancestors (Longhairs and American Shorthairs), but with the advantage of not needing such regular grooming as the genuine Longhair or Persian.

Coloring The undercoat is pure white and the coat heavily shaded with black to form a mantle over the spine, sides, and on the face and tail, gradually shading from very dark on the spine to white on the chin, chest, stomach, and under the tail. Legs are the same tone as the face. The general effect is much darker than the Chinchilla. Rims of the eyes, lips, and nose are outlined with black. Nose leather is brick red; paw pads are black. Eye color is green or blue-green.

Build Medium-sized and cobby, with a large, round head and small, low-set ears.

Temperament Sweet-natured and affectionate; generally undemanding.

Exotic Smoke

The Exotic Shorthair is the result of selective breeding between American Shorthairs and the best Longhairs or Persians. The cat is, therefore, Persian in type, with a cobby body and round, massive head, but the dense, soft coat is shorter and easier to groom. The eyes of this breed are a distinctive feature, being huge and wide set, with a sweet expression.

Litters of four are the average. The kittens are generally much darker than their parents, gaining their true colors only at maturity.

Coloring The Exotic Smoke may be of any color accepted in the Exotic Group, but instead of being sound in color from the tips to the roots of the coat, the base of each hair is silvery white. There must be no tabby markings, and the contrast between the top coat and the undercoat should be pronounced. The nose leather and paw pads should correspond with the coat color. The eye color should be copper, orange, or a deep gold.

Build Medium-sized and cobby, with a large, round head and small, low-set ears.

Temperament Sweet-natured and affectionate; generally undemanding.

Exotic Brown Tabby

Common standard faults in the Exotic Shorthair breed are a short or deformed tail, eyes that contrast with the coat coloring, and a head that is too small. Throughout the breed, the eyes should be large, round, and set well apart. The small, round-tipped ears are set both wide and low on the head.

Coloring Exotic tortoiseshell tabbies are accepted in brown, blue, chocolate, and lilac. The Exotic Spotted Tabby, in the same color range as the classic and mackerel tabbies, has numerous well-defined round, oval, or rosette-shaped marks, clearly etched in distinct color on the lighter base coat.

Build Medium-sized and cobby, with a large, round head and small, low-set ears.

Temperament Sweet-natured and affectionate; generally undemanding.

Exotic Silver Tabby

The Exotic Shorthair is accepted in the classic and mackerel patterns, but the intensity of the dark markings is reduced by the density of the coat when etched on a silver base coat. This cat has the brick-red nose leather desired for this variety.

Coloring The following colors are allowed: silver, brown, blue, chocolate, lilac, red, and cream. They have identical color requirements to the equivalent varieties in the British Shorthair, except for eye color, which in the Exotic Shorthair is brilliant copper.

Build Medium-sized and cobby, with a large, round head and small, low-set ears.

Temperament Sweet-natured and affectionate; generally undemanding.

Manx

Legends and fairy tales explaining the origins of this unique tail-less breed abound, but modern science agrees that its appearance is due to a mutant dominant gene. The original mutation must have occurred many years ago, for Manx cats have been known since 1900, with a specialist breed club being first established in Britain in 1901.

Although it is an old breed, Manx cats remain rare. The females produce small litters as a direct result of the gene for tail-lessness. This factor is actually a semi-lethal gene, and the homozygous Manx—one that inherits the tail-less gene from both parents—dies within the womb at an early stage of fetal development. The Manx that is born alive is therefore the heterozygote—one that inherits only one gene for tail-lessness, the other member of the gene pair being for a normal tail. Breeders usually cross tail-less Manx with normal-tailed Manx offspring to retain the correct body type.

The Manx's double coat repays good feeding and regular grooming. It should be combed through to the roots over the entire body and given a final sheen by polishing with the hands, a grooming mitt, or a silk scarf.

Coloring All colors and patterns are acceptable.
Build Medium-sized, with a round head and a straight, wide nose. The hind legs are longer than the front.
Temperament Intelligent, outgoing, and affectionate.

145

Tortoiseshell Manx

The Manx is accepted in many color varieties by most of the American associations. Each of the varieties listed has exactly the same color requirements as its equivalent in the American Shorthair, but with the exception of eye color. In American Shorthair varieties with brilliant gold eye color, the Manx should have eyes of brilliant copper.

The accepted varieties are: Black; Blue; Red; Cream; Tortoiseshell; Blue-cream; Calico; Dilute Calico; Chinchilla; Shaded Silver; Black Smoke; Blue Smoke; and Classic Mackerel and Tabby.

Coloring Any other color or pattern, with the exception of those showing hybridization resulting in the Colorpoint or Himalayan pattern. The eye color should be appropriate to the predominant color of the cat.

Build Medium-sized, with a round head and a straight, wide nose. The hind legs are longer than the front.

Temperament Intelligent, outgoing, and affectionate.

Scottish Fold

A litter of otherwise normal kittens born on a farm in Scotland contained the first Scottish Fold in 1961. A shepherd, William Ross, noticed the kitten with the quaint, folded ears and expressed an interest in acquiring such a cat. Two years later, the mother cat, Susie, gave birth to two kittens with folded ears, and William Ross was given one. A breeding program was begun in Britain, but when it was discovered that a small proportion of cats with folded ears also had thickened tails and limbs, the governing registration body banned Scottish Folds from all shows. The British breeders, who were dedicated to breeding only sound cats, resorted to registering their cats in overseas associations, and the main center of activity for the breed switched to the United States.

Today's Scottish Fold cats are bred to British Shorthairs in Britain and to American Shorthairs in the United States, or back to the prick-eared offspring of Folds. The folded ears are due to the action of a single dominant gene, and all Scottish Folds must have at least one fold-eared parent.

Coloring All colors are accepted. The eye color should be appropriate to the coat color, and each variety has identical color requirements to the equivalent variety in the American Shorthair.

Build Medium-sized and well rounded, with a flat skull and large, round eyes.

Temperament Sweet-natured and gentle; despite the curious ears, the breed has perfectly normal hearing.

Bicolor Scottish Fold

The short, dense coat is kept in good condition with the minimum of brushing and combing, and the folded ears are kept immaculate by gently cleaning inside the folds with a moistened cotton swab.

Coloring The color requirements for the Bicolor Scottish Fold are identical to the equivalent American Shorthair.
Build Medium-sized and well rounded, with a flat skull and large, round eyes.
Temperament Sweet-natured and gentle; despite the curious ears, the breed has perfectly normal hearing.

Calico Scottish Fold

The Scottish Fold is a loving, placid, and companionable cat, which loves both humans and other pets. The female makes a superb mother, and the kittens are quite precocious.

Coloring The color requirements for the Calico Scottish Fold are identical to the equivalent American Shorthair.
Build Medium-sized and well rounded, with a flat skull and large, round eyes.
Temperament Sweet-natured and gentle; despite the curious ears, the breed has perfectly normal hearing.

Snowshoe

The Snowshoe or Silver Laces is a rare cat, even in the United States where it was first bred. It combines the stocky build of the American Shorthair with the body length of the Siamese, and is Himalayan or Siamese in coloring, but with the white paws which are also found in the Birman.

Its coat needs the minimum of grooming, and the white paws may be kept immaculate by dusting with grooming powder from time to time to prevent discoloration.

Coloring Any recognized points color.
Build Medium-sized and well muscled, with a triangular face, large eyes, and rather pointed ears.
Temperament Sweet-natured, friendly, and intelligent.

FOREIGN SHORTHAIRED BREEDS

Abyssinian

No evidence exists to connect an Abyssinian cat, recorded as having been taken from Ethiopia to England in 1868, with today's pedigree cats. The modern Abyssinian is a well-established breed worldwide. It has been referred to as the Child of the Gods because of its close resemblance to the sacred cats of the ancient Egyptians. Whatever their color, all Abyssinian cats have unusual ticked coats, known as the agouti, or wild-type pattern. Selective breeding over many generations has resulted in a reduction of the natural tabby bars normally found on the face, neck, tail, and underparts, so that today's show cat has a clear, glowing, ticked coat, rather like that of a Belgian hare.

Coloring The Usual or Ruddy is the normal coat color for the Abyssinian, and is genetically black—the rich golden hairs having two or three bands of black ticking. The coat is warm ruddy brown with black ticking; the base color deep apricot or orange. The tail tip, ear tips, and eye rims are black; the nose leather brick red (may be outlined with black). Paw pads, back of feet, and toe tufts are seal brown or black. The eye color is gold or green; rich, deep colors are preferred.

Build Medium-sized, muscular, and lithe, with a slightly rounded wedge-shaped head with gentle contours.

Temperament Sweet-natured, very intelligent, and outgoing; will pine if deprived of company.

Blue Abyssinian

The coat is simple to keep immaculate with the minimum of grooming, and the large ears must be kept clean at all times, by regular use of moistened cotton swabs.

Coloring The coat is warm blue-gray with dark, steel blue-gray ticking; the base color pale fawn/cream. The tail tip and ear tips are dark steel blue-gray; the eye rims blue-gray. Nose leather is old rose (may be outlined with blue-gray); paw pads are old rose/blue-gray; backs of feet and toe tufts are deep steel blue-gray. Eye color is gold or green.

Build Medium-sized, muscular, and lithe, with a slightly rounded wedge-shaped head with gentle contours.

Temperament Sweet-natured, very intelligent, and outgoing; will pine if deprived of company.

Sorrel Abyssinian

The Abyssinian cat is typically quiet and gentle. It can be shy and rather reserved, mistrusting strangers, but it generally gets along well with other cats and adores its owner.

Coloring The Sorrel Abyssinian is also known as the Red Abyssinian. The coat is a bright, warm, copper red with chocolate-brown ticking; the base color deep apricot. The tail tip, ear tips, eye rims, backs of feet, and toe tufts are red-brown. Nose leather is pale red (may be outlined with red-brown); paw pads cinnamon to chocolate. Eye color is gold or green.

Build Medium-sized, muscular, and lithe, with a slightly rounded wedge-shaped head with gentle contours.

Temperament Sweet-natured, very intelligent, and outgoing; will pine if deprived of company.

Asian

The Asian group of cats encompasses a wide range of shorthaired breeds. All of the variants are of the Burmese type and basic conformation, but they do not have the Burmese coat color or slight restriction of color to the "points" areas as found in the usual Burmese cat.

Within this group is a range of cats with attractive coats for color pattern and texture. The fur is short and close-lying. All varieties of Asian cats have characteristically large, full, and expressive eyes, which are set well apart. They are slightly oriental in setting, but are neither Oriental nor round in shape.

Coloring Black, blue, chocolate, lilac, caramel, red, cream, apricot, and the associated tortoiseshell colors.

Build Medium-sized and well-muscled, but elegant, with a round-domed head.

Temperament Friendly, intelligent, playful, and lively.

Asian Tabby

Accepted in four different patterns—ticked, spotted, mackerel, and classic—and in all colors, this popular breed contains a sufficiently wide choice for even the most discerning of owners.

Each hair of the coat of the Ticked Tabby (shown here) is ticked with two or three bands of color, which produces the effect commonly seen in a wild rabbit. All cats of this variety should have clear tabby bars marking their legs and tail.

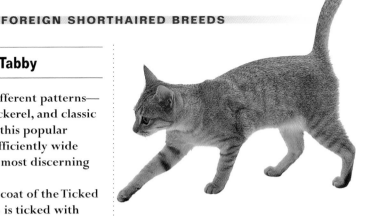

Coloring Black, blue, chocolate, lilac, caramel, red, cream, apricot, and the associated tortoiseshell colors, which are accepted in silver or standard versions and in full or Burmese expressions.

Build Medium-sized and well-muscled, but elegant, with a round-domed head.

Temperament Friendly, intelligent, playful, and lively.

Asian Smoke

The Smoke is another non-agouti cat with a pale, silvery, or near-white undercoat and darker top coat. Originally called the Burmoiré, the faint tabby markings give the impression of watered silk. The pale undercoat should reach one third to halfway up the hair shaft, the remaining part being darker. The forehead sometimes shows "frown" marks, and the eyes may be ringed in silver.

Coloring Black, blue, chocolate, lilac, caramel, red, cream, apricot, and the associated tortoiseshell colors.

Build Medium-sized and well-muscled, but elegant, with a round-domed head.

Temperament Friendly, intelligent, playful, and lively.

Bengal

Based on crosses between Asian Leopard Cats that live wild in Southeast Asia, and domestic cats, the Bengal was first produced in the United States. It seems to have preserved the self-assurance and confidence of the Asian Leopard Cat in conjunction with the affectionate disposition of the domestic cat, thus producing a miniature leopard with a loving nature. The appearance of the Bengal should be as close as possible to that of the first cross.

The texture of this breed's coat is unique, having the feel of satin or silk, and a glittering appearance as if sprinkled with gold dust or fragments of pearl. Its cooing or chirruping call is quite different from that of the ordinary domestic cat, which adds to the impression the ideal Bengal gives of being a truly wild cat.

In both the Leopard Spotted and Marble Patterned, the spectacles encircling the eyes should extend into vertical streaks, which may be outlined by an "M" on the forehead. A bold "chinstrap" and "mascara" markings, unbroken or broken necklets, and blotchy horizontal streaks are desirable in the Marble streaks, or spots in the Leopard.

Coloring The Marble (shown here) should have a distinct pattern with large swirled patches or streaks, clearly defined but not symmetrical, giving a marblelike impression, preferably with a horizontal flow. The pattern should be formed of distinct shapes and sharp outlines with sharp contrast between the base coat, and the markings should bear no similarity to that of the Classic Tabby.

Build Large-sized and muscular, with hindquarters slightly higher than the shoulders; a rounded head with small, round-tipped ears.

Temperament Friendly, intelligent, and inquisitive; an affectionate pet.

Leopard Spotted Bengal

Self-assured and as confident as its leopard cat ancestors, the Bengal has acquired an affectionate disposition and possesses a loving, dependable temperament.

The thick, luxuriant coat is kept in good condition with a well-balanced diet, and regular brushing and combing.

Coloring The Leopard Spotted should have generally large, well-formed, and randomly distributed spots. Extreme contrast between the ground color and the spots, which should be arrow-shaped, or rosetted in the case of larger spots. The cat's stomach must be spotted, and the legs may show broken horizontal lines and/or spots along its length with a solid dark-colored tip. It is important that the spots do not run vertically into a mackerel tabby pattern.

Build Large-sized and muscular, with the hindquarters slightly higher than the shoulders; a rounded head with small, round-tipped ears.

Temperament Friendly, intelligent, and inquisitive; an affectionate pet.

Snow Bengal

This variety shows the Burmese-Tonkinese coat pattern, in which the most intense color is at the points, but the pattern is still visible on the body and has a special glittering appearance.

In exhibitions, the Bengal is penalized for having a long, rough, or coarse coat, a ticked coat, incorrect color of the tail tip or paw pads, and an unspotted stomach.

Coloring The ground color is cream to light brown, with the overall appearance being that of a cat dusted with pearl glitter. The clearly visible pattern varies in color from charcoal to light brown; there are light-colored spectacles, whisker pads, and chin; and *ocelli* are preferred on each ear. The eye rims, lips, and nose leather are outlined in black; the center of the nose leather is brick red. The paw pads are rosy-toned brown; the tail tip is charcoal or dark brown. The eye color is gold, green, or blue-green.

Build Large-sized and muscular, with hindquarters slightly higher than the shoulders; a rounded head with small, round-tipped ears.

Temperament Friendly, intelligent, and inquisitive; an affectionate pet.

Bombay

Because of its looks, the Bombay cat has been referred to as the "patent-leather kid with new-penny eyes," an apt description for this shining jet-black feline. Developed from some outstandingly fine specimens of black American Shorthair and sable Burmese, the desired type was quickly achieved, and Bombays were found to breed true. Full recognition and championship status was granted by the CFA in 1976.

Although the cat looks like a black American-style Burmese, the early pioneers of the breed thought it looked like a miniature version of the Indian (Asian) black panther and so, after much deliberation, chose Bombay as the breed name.

The coat is easy to maintain with a balanced diet and minimal grooming. Buffing with a silk scarf or velvet grooming mitt enhances the typical patent-leather gloss.

Coloring Black only. Coat-jet black to the roots with a patent-leather sheen. Nose leather and paw pads are black. Eye color is gold to copper; the deeper shades are preferred.

Build Medium-sized and muscular, with a pleasantly round head and wide-set, round-tipped ears.

Temperament Affectionate, even-tempered, and playful; a good pet.

Burmese

All modern Burmese cats can trace their ancestry back to a Siamese hybrid female named Wong Mau, who was taken from Rangoon to the United States in 1930. Wong Mau was almost certainly a cat of the type known as Tonkinese today. At first she was mated with Siamese males; then her offspring were inter-mated, and some back-crossed to Wong Mau herself. From these matings three distinct types of kittens emerged— some identical to Wong Mau, some Siamese, and some much darker than Wong Mau. These cats were the foundation of the Burmese breed, which was officially recognized in 1936 by the Cat Fanciers' Association, and was the first breed of pedigree cats to be developed completely in the United States.

Coloring In some US associations, only the Sable (Brown) Burmese (shown here) is classed as a true Burmese. The rich, warm, sable brown coat shades almost imperceptibly to a lighter tone on the underparts, otherwise without any shading, barring, or markings of any kind. Kittens may be lighter in color. The nose leather and paw pads are brown. The eye color ranges from yellow to gold, with the deeper shades preferred.

Build Medium-sized and well-muscled but elegant, with a round-domed head and wide-set ears.

Temperament Intelligent, friendly, and outgoing; an affectionate pet.

Blue Burmese

A simple dilute of the usual brown color, the Blue Burmese was the first additional variety to be recognized and accepted. Standards for the ideal Burmese cat differ on each side of the Atlantic Ocean. The American Burmese has a rounder head and a slightly heavier body than its British counterpart. America's Burmese also tend to have better eye color, but as this breed was originally developed in the United States, this is probably to be expected. Eye color is very difficult to assess under the artificial light of a show hall, and judges often take Burmese entrants to a window with natural light if the eye color is at all suspect.

Coloring The coat is soft silver gray, very slightly darker on the back and tail. There should be a distinct silver sheen on the ears, face, and feet. Nose leather and paw pads are blue-gray. Eye color is yellow to gold.

Build Medium-sized and well-muscled but elegant, with a round-domed head and wide-set ears.

Temperament Intelligent, friendly, and outgoing; an affectionate pet.

Champagne Burmese

Also known as the Chocolate Burmese, this is one of the two new dilute colors of Burmese discovered in the USA in the late 1960s. It is now one of the most popular of all colors.

Coloring The warm milk-chocolate coat should be as even as possible, though the mask and ears may be very slightly deeper in color. Nose leather is chocolate brown; paw pads are cinnamon to chocolate brown; eye color is yellow to gold, with deeper shades preferred.

Build Medium-sized and well-muscled but elegant, with a round-domed head and wide-set ears.

Temperament Intelligent, friendly, and outgoing; an affectionate pet.

Cream Burmese

The Cream Burmese is a dilution of red and, together with this color, can produce the spectrum of tortoiseshell colors. The rich, pale cream coat makes a most attractive addition to the self-colored Burmese, and, like other paler colors, often shows a very slight Colorpoint or Himalayan effect, with darker color on the points—the face, ears, legs, paws, and tail.

Coloring The coat is pastel cream, with ears slightly darker than the body. Nose leather and paw pads are pink. Eye color is yellow to gold, with deeper shades preferred.

Build Medium-sized and well-muscled but elegant, with a round-domed head and wide-set ears.

Temperament Intelligent, friendly, and outgoing; an affectionate pet.

Platinum Burmese

Also known as the Lilac Burmese, this is the second of the two new dilute colors of Burmese discovered in the USA in the late 1960s, the other being the Champagne or Chocolate Burmese. These Burmese appeared in litters when cats that carried both the chocolate and blue color genes were mated together.

Coloring The pale delicate dove-gray coat has a pinkish tone, as even as possible, although the mask and ears may be very slightly deeper in color. Nose leather and paw pads are lavender-pink. Eye color is yellow to gold, with deeper shades preferred.

Build Medium-sized and well-muscled but elegant, with a round-domed head and wide-set ears.

Temperament Intelligent, friendly, and outgoing; an affectionate pet.

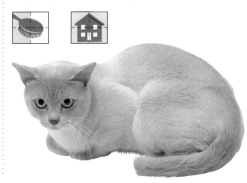

Red Burmese

The Burmese is a highly intelligent, active cat which can be strong willed, but repays firm, kind handling with affection.

Its short, glossy coat needs very little grooming to keep it in top condition.

Coloring The coat is actually a light tangerine color as even as possible, though very slight tabby markings are allowed on the face. Ears are darker than the body. Nose leather and paw pads are pink; eye color is yellow to gold, with deeper shades preferred.

Build Medium-sized and well-muscled but elegant, with a round-domed head and wide-set ears.

Temperament Intelligent, friendly, and outgoing; an affectionate pet.

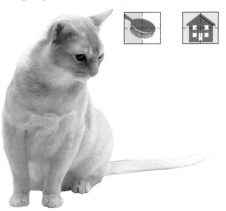

Tortoiseshell Burmese

The orange (red) gene was first introduced into the Burmese in Britain from three sources, a shorthaired ginger tabby, a red-pointed Siamese, and a calico domestic cat. A breeding program was set up, and by the mid-1970s, clear-coated red Burmese, cream Burmese, and the invariably female tortoiseshells had been produced in considerable numbers, most of which were of very good Burmese type.

In all varieties, the body color will be paler on the underparts than on the back and legs.

In non-tabby varieties, allowance is made in kittens and adolescent cats for an overall paler body color, and for faint tabby barring or ghost tabby markings. Tabby markings in adult cats of non-tabby varieties and white hairs are faults.

Coloring Tortoiseshell Burmese have mixed colors in their coats; there are four colors—brown, blue, chocolate, and lilac. In the Chocolate Tortoiseshell Burmese (shown here), the coat is milk chocolate, red and/or light red, patched and/or mottled. The nose leather and paw pads are plain or mottled, pink and/or blue-gray. The eye color is yellow to gold, with deeper shades preferred.

Build Medium-sized and well-muscled but elegant, with a round-domed head and wide-set ears.

Temperament Intelligent, friendly, and outgoing; an affectionate pet.

Burmilla

An accidental mating between a Platinum (Lilac) Burmese female and a Chinchilla Silver male in 1981 resulted in the birth of four black-shaded silver female kittens. All were of foreign conformation and had short, dense coats. They looked so spectacular and caused so much interest that similar matings were carried out. In 1983, the Cat Association of Britain accepted breeding programs and a standard of points for the breed.

The notable feature of the breed is the striking contrast between the pure silver undercoat and the shaded or tipped coat.

Coloring Shaded or tipped in black, blue, brown, chocolate, lilac, red, cream, red tortoiseshell, blue tortoiseshell, brown tortoiseshell, chocolate tortoiseshell, and lilac tortoiseshell. The Blue Shaded Burmilla (shown here) has a pure silver-white coat, shaded with blue-gray. The nose leather is brick red; the paw pads and soles are blue-gray. The eye color is green.

Build Medium-sized and athletic, with a gently rounded head with large, well-set eyes and broad-based, round-tipped ears.

Temperament Friendly, lively, intelligent, and affectionate; quieter and less demanding than the Burmese.

Shaded Burmilla

This elegant cat is of medium foreign type with a muscular body, long sturdy legs, and a moderately thick, long tail. The head is a medium wedge, with large ears, a short nose, and large expressive eyes. Its most impressive feature, however, is the sparkling coat. The ground color is pure silver white, with shading or tipping in any of the recognized solid or tortoiseshell colors, which must be uniformly distributed. The eyelids, lips, and nose leather are rimmed with the basic color, and delicate tracings of tabby markings are present on the points, which are more clearly defined on the shaded Burmilla than on the tipped varieties.

Coloring The coat of the Brown Shaded Burmilla is pure silver white, shaded with dark brown. The nose leather is brick red; the paw pads and soles are dark brown. The eye color is green.

Build Medium-sized and athletic, with a gently rounded head with large, well-set eyes and broad-based, round-tipped ears.

Temperament Friendly, lively, intelligent, and affectionate; quieter and less demanding than the Burmese.

Tipped Burmilla

The Burmilla is easy-going and relaxed, has a playful nature, and is very affectionate.

The dense coat is best groomed with a rubber brush to loosen dead hairs before being given a thorough combing.

The Burmilla male is larger and more stocky than the dainty female. Any tendency to the fine bone of the Siamese, or the cobby type of the Shorthair, is regarded as a fault.

Coloring The coat of the Black Tipped Burmilla is pure silver white, shaded or tipped with black. The nose leather is brick red; the paw pads and soles are black. The eye color is green.

Build Medium-sized and athletic, with a gently rounded head with large, well-set eyes and broad-based, round-tipped ears.

Temperament Friendly, lively, intelligent, and affectionate; quieter and less demanding than the Burmese.

Cornish Rex

In 1950 a curly-coated kitten was born in an otherwise normal litter at a farm in Cornwall in southwestern England. Microscopic examination of the kitten's hair samples showed they were similar to those of the Rex rabbit. When the kitten matured, he was mated with his mother, and two of the resulting three kittens had Rex coats. The male, Poldhu, eventually sired a stunning female called Lamorna Cover, which was exported to found the Cornish Rex breed in the United States. British Shorthairs and Burmese cats were used as foundation stock in the early days of Cornish Rex breeding, and eventually there were enough curly-coated cats to establish an acceptable breed. The Cornish Rex achieved full breed status in Britain in 1967 and in the United States in 1979.

The Cornish Rex cat is intelligent, affectionate, and rather extrovert by nature. Playful and mischievous, it makes a wonderful pet.

The unique curled coat does not shed hair, making is extremely easy to groom with hand stroking and the occasional use of a comb.

Coloring All coat colors and patterns are acceptable.

Build Medium-sized and slender, with a long, wedge-shaped head and large, very high-set ears.

Temperament Lively, intelligent, mischievous, and active.

Smoke Cornish Rex

The various colors and coat patterns of the cats selected for the original out-crosses resulted in a wide range of color varieties in the Cornish Rex. Whatever the color, however, the short plush coat is dense and has uniform narrow waves extending from the top of the head, across the back, sides, and hips, and continuing to the tip of the tail, which must be long, fine, and tapered, as well as being well covered with waved fur.

Coloring All coat colors and patterns are acceptable.

Build Medium-sized and slender, with a long, wedge-shaped head and large, high-set ears.

Temperament Lively, intelligent, mischievous, and active.

Tortoiseshell Cornish Rex

In exhibition, the Cornish Rex is penalized for having a shaggy coat or one that is too short. They should not have a head of the Shorthair type, and the ears must be large.

Offspring of Cornish Rex to non-rexed cats result in cats with normal coats, carrying the recessive gene for the curly coat. When they are mature and mated with similar cats, or back to a Cornish Rex, curly-coated kittens are produced.

Coloring All coat colors and patterns are acceptable.

Build Medium-sized and slender, with a long, wedge-shaped head and large, high-set ears.

Temperament Lively, intelligent, mischievous, and active.

Devon Rex

Ten years after the discovery of the first Cornish Rex kitten, another curly-coated kitten was discovered in the neighboring English county of Devon. The kitten, named Kirlee, was eventually mated with some Cornish Rex queens. To everyone's surprise, all the resulting kittens were flat-coated, and it was concluded that Kirlee's curls were caused by a different gene. More breeding tests confirmed this.

The two rex-coated varieties were developed quite separately and are quite distinct breeds. The Devon Rex would look rather unusual even without its wavy coat, having a quizzical, pixie-like expression, and huge bat-like ears.

In Britain, a popular sub-variety of Devon Rex is known unofficially as the Si-Rex. It combines all of the characteristics of the typical Devon Rex with the Siamese coat pattern and colors.

Coloring All coat colors and patterns are acceptable.

Build Medium-sized and well-muscled, but slender, with a wedge-shaped head and large, low-set ears.

Temperament Mischievous, playful, intelligent, and friendly.

Tortoiseshell Devon Rex

The Devon is said to be the cat for the connoisseur. It is demanding as a pet, constantly craving human attention, loving, playful, and intelligent.

The cat is very easy to groom with hand stroking and occasional combing. It often shows sparse areas on the body, and when it does, the cat needs extra warmth. The large ears need regular cleaning.

Coloring All feline colors are accepted, including white markings, which are disallowed in other varieties.

Build Medium-sized and well-muscled, but slender, with a wedge-shaped head and large, low-set ears.

Temperament Mischievous, playful, intelligent, and friendly.

Colorpoint Devon Rex

Like the Cornish Rex, the first Devons were out-crossed to cats of other foreign breeds in order to widen the gene pool of available breeding stock. Siamese cats were extensively used, and the resulting curled cats were called Si-Rex in the beginning. Si-Rex is not now accepted as correct terminology for the Siamese-patterned Devon Rex, and white markings are not permitted in cats with the Himalayan or Siamese coat pattern, where the color is restricted to the cat's points.

Coloring All coat colors and patterns recognized in the feline standards for Colorpoints are acceptable.

Build Medium-sized and well-muscled, but slender, with a wedge-shaped head and large, low-set ears.

Temperament Mischievous, playful, intelligent, and friendly.

Egyptian Mau

Not to be confused with cats of the same name bred experimentally in Britain during the 1960s and now called Oriental Tabbies, the Egyptian Mau was bred in the United States, and came from foundation stock brought there from Egypt via Rome in 1953. A spotted cat, very similar to those pictured in ancient Egyptian scrolls and cartoons, it gained official recognition from the CFF in 1968 and finally from the CFA in 1977.

Rather shy but very loving, the Mau tends to attach its affections to only one or two people. It is naturally active and may easily be taught one or two tricks.

Although the short coat is easy to keep in good condition, regular combing is required to remove dead hair.

In addition to the Silver Mau (shown here), there are Bronze and Smoke Maus.

Coloring Pale silver ground color; dark charcoal markings contrasting with ground color. Backs of the ears are grayish pink tipped in black; the nose, lips, and eyes are outlined in black. The upper throat, chin, and around the nostrils is pale clear silver, appearing white. Nose leather is brick red; paw pads are black. Eye color is light green.

Build Medium-sized, long, and graceful with a slightly rounded wedge-shaped head and fairly large ears.

Temperament Highly intelligent, companionable, adventurous, and outgoing.

Havana Brown

Also known as the Oriental Chestnut, this unique, manmade breed came into being when British breeders were working with Russian Blue and Shorthair cross-matings during the early 1950s, and self-colored chocolate brown kittens were occasionally produced. At that time, the science of feline color genetics was in its infancy, but it was soon established that chocolate kittens could occur only when both parents carried the chocolate factor, and when two chocolate cats were mated, chocolate kittens always resulted.

Cats from these early matings were out-crossed to Siamese to establish Oriental type and conformation. Others were sent to the United States and were bred to a unique standard of points.

The breed is highly intelligent, affectionate, and very agile. Less vocal than the Siamese, it is playful and craves human company. It makes a superb pet.

The coat is easy to maintain in good condition with the minimum of grooming. Combing removes any loose hairs, and buffing with the hand or a silk scarf produces a sheen on the glossy brown coat.

Coloring Warm brown only. The nose leather is brown with a rosy flush; the paw pads must have a rosy tone. The eye color is a vivid green.

Build Medium-sized and muscular, but slim and elegant, with a wedge-shaped head.

Temperament Intelligent, affectionate, and companionable.

Japanese Bobtail

A natural breed, which has existed in its native Japan for centuries, the Japanese Bobtail is considered to be a symbol of good luck in the home, and the tricolored variety, known as the *mi-ke* (meaning three colors), is particularly favored.

The Bobtail first came to the attention of cat fanciers in the Western world when an American cat show judge visiting Japan became captivated by the breed, and Bobtails were accepted for provisional status by the CFA in May 1971.

After five years of careful breeding, the Japanese Bobtail became well established in the United States and gained full recognition and Championship Status.

The silky coat is easy to maintain in perfect condition with gentle brushing and combing, finishing with the hands or a silk scarf. The pompom on the tail is combed into shape, and the wide ears are kept in pristine condition by wiping daily with a cotton swab.

Coloring Typically tortoiseshell and white, but other colors are acceptable.
Build Medium-sized, lean, and well-muscled.
Temperament Friendly, intelligent, and very companionable, with an endearing personality.

Korat

The breed originated in Thailand, where it is called Si-Sawat, which is a descriptive compound word referring to its silver gray coat and luminous, light green eyes. Highly prized in its native land, the Si-Sawat is considered a harbinger of good fortune, and a pair of these cats is a traditional wedding gift, intended to bring longevity, wealth, and happiness to the couple.

The Korat is a dainty, quiet-voiced little cat, generally alert, inquisitive, and affectionate.

Its short, dense coat is easily cared for with a weekly brushing and buffing with a silk scarf.

Coloring Blue only. Nose leather and lips are dark blue or lavender; paw pads are dark blue ranging to lavender with a pinkish tinge. The eye color is luminous green, although amber is acceptable.

Build Medium-sized and muscular, with a heart-shaped face and large ears which are round-tipped.

Temperament Quiet, intelligent, playful, and affectionate; a loving pet.

Malayan

This very recent breed originated in the United States, where it was officially recognized in 1980. It differs from the Burmese only in its color, and it is in fact classed as Burmese in the UK. Malayan kittens are regularly and naturally produced as part of Burmese litters.

The fur is short, fine, and soft, and it is best groomed by stroking with a gloved hand.

Coloring There are three color forms. The Blue Malayan is blue-gray with a fawn hint; the Platinum is silver-gray with a fawn hint; the Champagne form (shown here) is yellow brown. Eye color is yellow in all the forms.

Build Hard and muscular with a strong, rounded chest; the round eyes are wide set.

Temperament Extremely affectionate and outgoing; a good family pet but demands attention.

Ocicat

The first kitten of this breed appeared in the litter of an experimentally bred hybrid queen, from an Abyssinian-pointed Siamese breeding program, mated with a chocolate-pointed Siamese male. The kitten, which was called Tonga, reminded its breeder of a baby ocelot, and she decided to produce similar cats, which were eventually recognized as a separate breed called Ocicats.

Apart from the Ocicat itself, out-crosses to Abyssinian, American, and Siamese are allowed in the pedigree. The Ocicat is a rather large, but well-proportioned cat, muscular and agile, with a typically "wild-cat" appearance.

Their coats are groomed by gentle brushing and combing through on a regular basis to remove dead hair.

Coloring Black, blue, chocolate, lavender, cinnamon, fawn spots, or silver variations of these colors. All colors should be clear, with the lightest color on the face, around the eyes, on the chin, and the lower jaw. The darkest color at the tail's tip. Eye color is golden.

Build Solid and well-muscled, with a broad head and muzzle and large, wide-set ears.

Temperament Intelligent, friendly, and companionable; a good family pet.

Russian Blue

The very handsome and distinctive Russian Blue is a natural breed with a unique combination of conformation, color, and coat that makes it such a striking animal.

The first Russian Blue cats are thought to have originated near the White Sea port of Archangel, just outside the Arctic Circle. The cats were shown extensively in England during the latter part of the nineteenth century, but differed from those of today in having bright orange eyes. In 1912, the Russian Blue was given its own classes, but during World War II, the breed almost became extinct, being saved only by out-crossing to Siamese. Cats of foreign type were then shown as Russian Blues, but eventually breeders made a coordinated attempt to return to the prewar characteristics of the breed, and in 1966 the show standard was changed to state specifically that Siamese type was undesirable in the Russian Blue.

Coloring A clear even blue, with silver-tipped guard hairs, giving an overall lustrous silvery sheen. Nose leather is slate gray; paw pads are lavender-pink or mauve. The eye color is vivid green.

Build Medium-sized, lithe, and muscular, with a flat-skulled wedge-shaped head and wide-based ears.

Temperament Quiet, gentle, highly intelligent, and affectionate.

Singapura

An American cat breeder developed the Singapura from cats she discovered in Singapore. She decided to import some into the United States, and drew up a careful program for the development of the breed. Her work has been rewarded by the production of an attractive, viable feline breed with considerable esthetic appeal. The Singapura has a ticked coat, similar to that of the Abyssinian, and is of moderate Foreign Shorthair bone structure and conformation.

Coloring The ground color is warm ivory; the ticking is dark brown. The muzzle, chin, chest, and stomach are the color of unbleached cheesecloth; the ears and bridge of the nose are salmon toned. The nose leather is pale to dark salmon pink, outlined with dark brown; the paw pads are rosy brown; the eye rims are dark brown. The eye color is hazel, green, or yellow.
Build Small to medium-sized, with a rounded head and large, pointed ears.
Temperament Affectionate, friendly, and playful.

Somali

This breed is the longhaired version of the Abyssinian cat, and its coat color is typically Abyssinian. It was thought that the long coat was due to a spontaneous mutation occurring within the Abyssinian breed, but genetic investigation showed that the gene for long hair was probably introduced when cats of Abyssinian type and lineage were out-crossed to others in the early days of breeding and showing.

When the first longcoated kittens appeared in otherwise normal litters of Abyssinian kittens, they were discarded and given away as pets, but later breeders decided to develop the longhaired Abyssinian as a separate variety.

Although different cat associations have their own rules for acceptance of new varieties, the Somali is recognized in most of the regular Abyssinian color varieties by most registering bodies.

Coloring The coat is a warm ruddy brown with black ticking; the base color is deep apricot or orange. The tail tip, ear tips, and eye rims are black. The nose leather is brick red (sometimes outlined with black); the paw pads, back of feet, and toe tufts are seal brown or black. The eye color is gold or green; rich deep colors are preferred.

Build Medium-sized to large, well-proportioned, and muscular, with a moderately wedge-shaped head.

Temperament Intelligent, outgoing, and companionable.

Non-silver Chocolate Somali

The Cat Association of Britain accepts all colors of Somali, while the GCCF has granted full Championship status to the Usual and Sorrel in the Non-silver group, and has given preliminary status only to the blue, chocolate, lilac, and fawn non-Silvers, and to all the Silver Somali cats in the full range of colors.

Coloring The coat is rich golden coppery brown ticked with dark chocolate, with paler base hair. The ears and tail are tipped with the same shade as the ticking. The nose leather is pinkish chocolate, paw pads are chocolate, darker between the toes and up the heels. Toe tufts are dark chocolate.

Build Medium-sized to large, well-proportioned, and muscular, with a moderately wedge-shaped head.

Temperament Intelligent, outgoing, and companionable.

Non-silver Fawn Somali

A diluted version of the Red or Sorrel Somali, the Fawn has an attractive "powdered" effect to its warm fawn coat, ticked with a deeper fawn color.

Coloring The warm fawn coat is ticked with a deeper shade of the same color and a paler base coat; ears and tail are tipped with same color as ticking and nose leather is pink. Pinkish-mauve paw pads are deep fawn between the toes and up the heels. The toe tufts are deep fawn.

Build Medium-sized to large, well-proportioned, and muscular, with a moderately wedge-shaped head.

Temperament Intelligent, outgoing, and companionable.

Silver Somali

A yellowish effect on the body, known as "fawning," is an undesirable trait in the Silver series of Somali cats. It occurs particularly in the usual silver, and in blue silver varieties especially on the face and paws.

Coloring The white base coat is ticked with black; the tail and ears are tipped with black. The nose leather is light brick red. The paw pads are black or brown with black between the toes and extending up the heels with black toe tufts.

Build Medium-sized to large, well-proportioned, and muscular, with a moderately wedge-shaped head.

Temperament Intelligent, outgoing, and companionable.

Red Silver Somali

The Red Somali is also known as the Sorrel Somali. Like the Abyssinian, the Somali is gentle and receptive to quiet handling and affection. It is soft-voiced, playful, and athletic, and makes a perfect companion pet. The coat, though full, is not

wooly and is therefore every easy to groom. The full frill (ruff) and tail need regular combing through, and the large ears must be gently cleaned and kept free from dust.

Coloring The white base coat has chocolate ticking, giving the overall sparkling silvery peach effect. The ears and tail are tipped with chocolate. The nose leather is pink. The pink paw pads have chocolate brown between the toes and extending up the heels. The toe tufts are dark chocolate.

Build Medium-sized to large, well-proportioned, and muscular, with a moderately wedge-shaped head.

Temperament Intelligent, outgoing, and companionable.

Sphynx

Although it appears so, the Sphynx is not truly hairless. The skin has the texture of soft leather and may be covered with a fine down, which is almost imperceptible to the eye. A fine covering of hair is sometimes apparent on the ears, muzzle, feet, tail, and scrotum.

The first Sphynx appeared as a spontaneous mutation in a litter born to a black and white domestic cat in Ontario, Canada, in 1966. A breeder of Siamese cats took the hairless kitten, and with other breeders worked on the development of a new breed. Today the Sphynx is accepted by only a few feline associations, and it remains a rare and unique breed.

People-orientated and not fond of other cats, the Sphynx does not like being held or strongly petted. It often stands with one foreleg raised, and resists lying with its body touching the ground, preferring a warm surface.

It never needs brushing, but the suede-like body must be kept in good condition by hand grooming and rubbing down with a soft cloth.

Coloring All colors and patterns are acceptable; white lockets and buttons are also accepted.

Build Medium-sized and muscular, with long, slim legs, a slender neck, and a head that is longer than it is wide.

Temperament Friendly, outgoing, and intelligent.

ORIENTAL
BREEDS

Balinese

The longcoated kittens that appeared from time to time in otherwise normal litters of Siamese cats were developed into the Balinese. At first such kittens were quickly discarded and sold as pets, but in the 1940s two breeders in New York and California began to work toward the development of a separate breed. The name was chosen because of the cats' gracefulness and svelte lines, reminiscent of the dancers on the island of Bali.

The long coat is nothing like that of the Persian. It has no wooly undercoat and lies flat against the body. The coat is relatively easy to care for with regular gentle combing, and brushing of the frill (ruff) and plumed tail.

As might be expected from their ancestry, Balinese are very similar to Siamese in character—affectionate, demanding of attention, extremely active, and inquisitive.

Coloring All colors found in the Siamese and other Colorpoints: seal, blue, chocolate, lilac, red, and cream, as well as tortoiseshell and tabby forms of these colors. Some associations accept only seal point, blue point, chocolate point, and lilac point.

Build Medium-sized, svelte, and elegant, with a long, tapering, wedge-shaped head and large, pointed ears.

Temperament Lively and intelligent, but slightly quieter and less boisterous than the Siamese.

Blue Colorpoint Balinese

The body must be even in color with subtle shading when allowed in the color variety. The points—mask, ears, legs, feet, and tail—must be all the same shade and clearly defined. The mask should cover the entire face, including the whisker pads, and be connected to the ears by traced markings. There should be no ticking or white hairs in the points.

Coloring The body color is bluish-white of a glacial tone. The points are blue-gray. The nose leather and paw pads are blue-gray. The eye color is a deep, vivid blue.

Build Medium-sized, svelte, and elegant, with a long, tapering, wedge-shaped head and large, pointed ears.

Temperament Lively and intelligent, but slightly quieter and less boisterous than the Siamese.

Seal Tabby Colorpoint Balinese

A longcoated version of the Siamese, it is accepted in the same range of point colors. As only top-quality Siamese cats were used in the breeding program, most of today's Balinese are of outstanding type. The Seal Tabby Colorpoint epitomizes the best qualities of the breed.

Coloring The body color is beige; the points color is dark seal tabby. The rims around the eyes and the nose are seal brown. The nose leather is brick red, pink, or seal brown; the paw pads are seal brown. The eye color is deep, vivid blue.

Build Medium-sized, svelte, and elegant, with a long, tapering, wedge-shaped head and large, pointed ears.

Temperament Lively and intelligent, but slightly quieter and less boisterous than the Siamese.

Colorpoint Shorthair

When Siamese cats were mated with cats of other varieties, such as the tabby shorthair, in order to achieve new colors and patterns, the Colorpoint Shorthair was the result. Because the gene that restricts the color to the points in Siamese is recessive, the resulting kittens were colored all over.

When these cross-bred cats were mated back to high-quality Siamese, however, Siamese-patterned offspring were produced, and successive back-crossing to Siamese upgraded the "new" Siamese to conform to the rigorous standards set by various associations.

Siamese in everything but name, the Colorpoint Shorthair is a delightfully intelligent, agile, and affectionate pet. It is very easy to maintain in top condition by feeding a good diet and needs minimal grooming, just combing through to remove any dead hair and buffing the fine coat either with the hands or a silk scarf.

Coloring Points in red, cream, seal lynx, blue lynx, chocolate lynx, lilac lynx, red lynx, seal torbie, chocolate torbie, blue-cream, and lilac-cream.

Build Medium-sized, svelte, and dainty.

Temperament Intelligent, affectionate, and agile; an ideal pet.

Chocolate Tortie Colorpoint Shorthair

Siamese cats under a different title in some American associations, the Colorpoint Shorthair group embraces all the Siamese varieties produced by out-crossing to other breeds to introduce the orange (red) and tabby genes.

Coloring The body is ivory and may be mottled in older cats. The points are warm milk chocolate uniformly mottled with red and/or light red. A blaze is desirable. Nose leather is cinnamon; flesh or coral mottling is permitted where there is a facial blaze. Paw pads are cinnamon; flesh or coral mottling is permitted where the points' color mottling extends into the paw pads. Eye color is a deep, vivid blue.

Build Medium-sized, svelte, and dainty.

Temperament Intelligent, affectionate, and agile; an ideal pet.

Javanese

The longhaired Oriental, now known as the Javanese, was selectively bred from Oriental cats and longcoated cats of exceptional Oriental type. In the CFA, the name Javanese was given to Balinese cats not conforming to the four main Siamese colors (seal point, blue point, chocolate point, and lilac point). These were the red- and tabby-based colors which in the shortcoated varieties are termed Colorpoints by the CFA.

Medium long on the body, and without an undercoat, the coat of the Javanese cat is fine, with a silky texture. It flows over the body and forms a frill (ruff) around the shoulders and chest. The cat has a full, plume-like tail.

Regular gentle brushing keeps the coat in good condition; the frill (ruff), underparts and tail can be combed gently with a wide-toothed comb.

Coloring As for the Oriental Shorthair: black, blue, chocolate, lilac, red, cream, cinnamon, fawn, tortoiseshell (all colors), smoke (all colors), tabby (all colors), tabby-tortoiseshell (all colors). The eye color for all forms is vivid, intense green.

Build Medium-sized, svelte, and elegant.

Temperament Alert, extrovert, active, and inquisitive; an affectionate family pet.

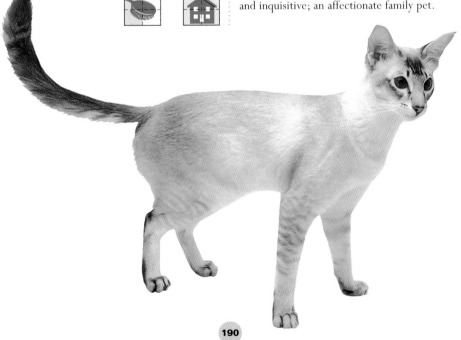

Oriental

Black Oriental

Although it is recorded that a solid black cat of Siamese type existed in Germany just before World War II, it was not until the early 1960s in Britain that thought was given to setting up a breeding program to produce a self-colored Siamese. These cats are now known as Orientals, and the Black is one of the most eye catching and elegant of all, with its short, glossy, and close-lying coat and long, slender body.

They are naturally very clean cats, and the very short, fine coat can be kept in good condition with daily hand grooming and buffing with a silk scarf. The large ears need regular cleaning, and Orientals should be provided with a scratching post and plenty of toys to play with.

Coloring The coat color is dense coal black, sound from the roots to the tips of the hair, free from any rusty tinge, and without any white hairs or other markings. There should be no gray undercoat. The nose leather is black; the paw pads are black or seal brown. The eye color is vivid, an intense green.

Build Medium-sized, long, slim, and elegant, with a Siamese-type, wedge-shaped head and large, wide-set ears.

Temperament Companionable, intelligent, inquisitive, and very attention-seeking.

Blue Oriental

As Siamese cats without the gene that restricts the color to the points, the first Orientals to appear in half-Siamese litters were blacks and blues. Later, the elusive chocolate gene produced a self-chocolate-colored cat, and when the gene for dilution was also present in the cats used for breeding, lilac or lavender kittens began to appear.

Coloring The coat color is any shade of blue-gray, but lighter shades are preferred. The color must be sound and even throughout, without any white hairs, shadings, or other markings. Nose leather and paw pads are blue-gray. The eye color is vivid, intense green.

Build Medium-sized, long, slim, and elegant, with a Siamese-type, wedge-shaped head and large, wide-set ears.

Temperament Companionable, intelligent, inquisitive, and attention-seeking.

Cinnamon Oriental

This beautiful and unusual color variety excited geneticists when it first appeared. It is the result of introducing the sorrel gene from the Siamese to Abyssinian matings. The dilute version of this warm, rather unusual cinnamon-brown color is known as Fawn.

Coloring The coat color is warm cinnamon brown, sound and even throughout without any white hairs, shadings, or markings. The nose leather is cinnamon brown; the paw pads are cinnamon brown to pink. The eye color is vivid, intense green.

Build Medium-sized, long, slim, and elegant, with a Siamese-type, wedge-shaped head and large, wide-set ears.

Temperament Companionable, intelligent, inquisitive, and attention-seeking.

Cream Oriental

Cream is one of the newer colors, and it is a dilute version of Red. This form has proved to be a useful addition to breeding programs, because when a Cream is mated to a Caramel, it can produce apricot-colored cats.

Tabby markings may be evident in the coat of the Cream Oriental, and an otherwise good cat will not be penalized for this excusable fault.

Coloring The coat color is pale, pure pastel cream, with no warm tone, sound and even throughout without any white hairs, shadings, or markings. There must be no light or white undercoat. The nose leather and paw pads are pink; the preferred eye color is vivid, intense green. Note: Slight shading is allowed on the face and legs, and dark whiskers are permitted.

Build Medium-sized, long, slim, and elegant, with a Siamese-type, wedge-shaped head and large, wide-set ears.

Temperament Companionable, intelligent, inquisitive, and attention-seeking.

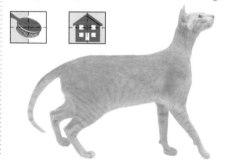

Lilac Oriental

The Lilac Oriental, which is sometimes known as the Lavender Oriental, was one of the first varieties to be developed.

Like other Orientals, it is extroverted, intelligent, and very affectionate with its own family and friends. It is active and playful, and hates being left alone for long periods.

Coloring The coat color is faded lilac with a slight pinkish tinge, sound and even throughout without any white hairs, shadings, or other markings. The nose leather and paw pads are lavender-pink or faded lilac. The eye color is vivid, intense green.

Build Medium-sized, long, slim, and elegant, with a Siamese-type, wedge-shaped head and large, wide-set ears.

Temperament Companionable, intelligent, inquisitive, and attention-seeking.

Red Oriental

The type of the Oriental is exactly the same as the Siamese. In fact, Oriental cats are merely Siamese without the gene that restricts the color to the points of the body. With the loss of the Himalayan factor, comes the change of eye color from blue to green.

Coloring The coat color is deep, rich, clear and brilliant red, sound and even throughout, without any white hairs, lighter shadings, or markings. The nose leather and paw pads are brick red or pink. The eye color is vivid, intense green. Note: Slight shading is allowed on the face and legs, and dark whiskers are permitted.

Build Medium-sized, long, slim, and elegant, with a Siamese-type, wedge-shaped head and large, wide-set ears.

Temperament Companionable, intelligent, inquisitive, and attention-seeking.

White Oriental

The only Oriental color without green eyes, the White is glacial white with blue eyes. Unusually for this group, it is not often mated to other Orientals, but to Siamese, because this ensures the correct blue eye color. In some associations it is known as the Foreign White.

Coloring The coat color is pure white without markings or shadings of any kind. The nose leather and paw pads are pink. The eye color is deep, vivid blue. Note: In the CFA, the Oriental White should have green eyes. Blue eye color is also accepted, but odd-eyed cats are not.

Build Medium-sized, long, slim, and elegant, with a Siamese-type, wedge-shaped head and large, wide-set ears.

Temperament Companionable, intelligent, inquisitive, and attention-seeking.

Black Smoke Oriental

In the Smoke, the hairs are tipped with the appropriate color and have a narrow silver-white band at the roots which can only be seen when the hair is parted. The undercoat is silver-white. In repose, the cat appears to be of solid color, but when it is in motion the silver-white undercoat is clearly visible.

Coloring The hairs are tipped with black. Nose leather and paw pads are black. The eye color is green.

Build Medium-sized, long, slim, and elegant, with a Siamese-type, wedge-shaped head and large, wide-set ears.

Temperament Companionable, intelligent, inquisitive, and attention-seeking.

Chocolate Silver Shaded Oriental

The introduction of silver to the Oriental breeding programs excited many Oriental fanciers, and before long, cats with short, fine silvery-white coats were bred with various amounts of colored tipping. The most heavily tipped are the Smokes, the lightest tipped are just called Tipped, and the intermediates are known as Shaded.

In the Shaded, the hair is tipped to about one third of its length and the undercoat is white, producing the characteristic sparkling appearance of this color group. The face and legs may be shaded with tipping.

Coloring Chocolate markings on a paler, silvery chocolate ground. The eye color is green.

Build Medium-sized, long, slim, and elegant, with a Siamese-type, wedge-shaped head and large, wide-set ears.

Temperament Companionable, intelligent, inquisitive, and attention-seeking.

Chocolate Classic Tabby Oriental

Oriental Tabby cats may have any of the following four tabby patterns—classic, mackerel, spotted, or ticked.

In the classic, there should be dense and clearly defined broad markings; the legs should be evenly barred with bracelets coming up to join the body markings. The tail should be evenly ringed; there should be several unbroken necklaces on the neck and upper chest. Frown marks on the forehead form a letter "M."

Coloring The base coat, including the lips and chin, is warm fawn, with markings a rich, chocolate brown. The backs of the legs from paw to heel are chocolate brown; the nose leather is chocolate or pale red rimmed with chocolate; the paw pads are cinnamon to chocolate; the eyes are green.

Build Medium-sized, long, slim, and elegant, with a Siamese-type, wedge-shaped head and large, wide-set ears.

Temperament Companionable, intelligent, inquisitive, and attention-seeking.

Chocolate Ticked Tabby Oriental

Matings between Siamese and Abyssinians introduced the gene for ticking into the Oriental Tabby breeding program and so gave rise to the Oriental Ticked Tabby. With its evenly ticked coat, reminiscent of its wild-cat ancestors, it soon became a popular pattern.

The body hairs should be clearly ticked with two or three bands of ticking on each hair, but there are no other spots, bars, or stripes on the body. The basic color shows at the heels of the hind legs and at the tip of the tail. Typical tabby markings, including the forehead "M," are found on the face, and thumb-prints are seen on the backs of the ears.

Coloring The base coat, including the lips and chin, is sandy beige, with markings a rich, chocolate brown. The backs of the legs, from paw to heel, are chocolate brown. The nose leather is chocolate or pale red rimmed with chocolate; the paw pads are cinnamon to chocolate. The eye color is green.

Build Medium-sized, long, slim, and elegant, with a Siamese-type, wedge-shaped head and large, wide-set ears.

Temperament Companionable, intelligent, inquisitive, and attention-seeking.

Silver Spotted Tabby Oriental

The first recognized tabby pattern in the Oriental section, the Spotted Tabby was first seen in the late 1960s. Until 1978, it was known in the UK as the Egyptian Mau, but its name was changed to avoid confusion with the American breed of that name, which is entirely unrelated and quite different.

The spots on the body may vary in size and shape, but those that are round and evenly distributed are preferred. They must not run together to form a broken mackerel pattern. A dorsal stripe runs the length of the body to the tip of the tail and is ideally composed of spots.

Coloring The base coat, including the lips and chin, is pure pale silver, with dense black markings. The backs of the legs from paw to heel are black; the nose leather is black or brick red with black rims; paw pads are black. The eye color is green.

Build Medium-sized, long, slim, and elegant, with a Siamese-type, wedge-shaped head and large, wide-set ears.

Temperament Companionable, intelligent, inquisitive, and attention-seeking.

Tortoiseshell Oriental

With the introduction of the sex-linked gene that produced the Red and Cream Orientals, litters included female kittens in various other combinations of colors in the pattern called tortoiseshell. The base color in all Tortoiseshell Oriental cats must be sound to the roots, patched or mingled with red, cream, or rich beige, and totally free from tabby markings.

As with most tortoiseshell cats, the Orientals are usually female only, although the rare, fertile male is occasionally seen.

Coloring Tortoiseshell Orientals are seen in black, blue, chocolate, lilac (lavender), cinnamon, and caramel. The nose leather and paw pads should be the appropriate color for the standard. The eye color is green.

Build Medium-sized, long, slim, and elegant, with a Siamese-type, wedge-shaped head and large, wide-set ears.

Temperament Companionable, intelligent, inquisitive, and attention-seeking.

Seychellois

Following a breeding program approved by the Cat Association of Britain, the Seychellois was developed by a small group of breeders interested in Oriental cats. It is of medium size and typical Oriental conformation, with a long, svelte body, slim legs, and dainty paws. The head is wedge-shaped with very large pointed ears and distinctive almond-shaped eyes.

It is unusual in having a predominantly white coat, with splashes of color on the head, legs, and body, and a colored tail. Seychellois markings are classified into three groups. The Seychellois Longhair is identical in every respect to the Shorthair except in its coat, which is of medium length, soft, and silky in texture, and longer on the frill (ruff). It has ear tufts and and a full, plume-like tail.

Coloring Any color or combination of colors is allowed.
Build Medium-sized, long, and svelte.
Temperament Intelligent, affectionate, agile, and inquisitive.

Siamese

Probably the best known of all pedigree breeds, the Siamese cat of today is quite different from that seen in the early 1900s, although it still retains its points, caused by the Himalayan factor, the gene that restricts the true coloring to the animal's face, ears, legs, paws, and tail.

Seal-pointed cats were presented by the Royal Court of Siam to British and American diplomats toward the end of the nineteenth century, and the breed gained public interest, which has continued to grow.

Although the original Royal Cats of Siam were seal-pointed, some had lighter brown points, and these were recognized as Chocolate Points. A naturally occurring dilute factor also became apparent when the almost black coloration of the seal point gave rise to cats with slate-gray extremities. These were eventually accepted as the color variety Blue Point.

With increasing knowledge of feline color genetics, breeders of Siamese cats realized that they could increase the range of color varieties by first making judicious out-crosses, then back-breeding the offspring to Siamese of excellent type. The red series of points colors was added by out-crossing to red, red tabby, and tortoiseshell cats, and a range of colors in tabby-pointed cats was developed from out-crosses with tabbies.

Coloring Points in seal (shown here), blue, chocolate, lilac, red, cream, seal torbie, blue torbie, chocolate torbie, lilac torbie, seal tabby, blue tabby, chocolate tabby, lilac tabby, red tabby, cream tabby, seal torbie tabby, blue torbie tabby, chocolate torbie tabby, lilac torbie tabby. The eyes of all varieties are deep, vivid blue.

Build Medium-sized, long, slim, and athletic, with a long, flat-profiled, wedge-shaped head and large, wide-set ears.

Temperament Lively, intelligent, and inquisitive; demands attention and has a loud voice.

Blue Point Siamese

The Blue Point made its debut at a show in 1896, but was originally regarded as a poorly colored Seal Point. The body must be even in color with subtle shading when allowed in the color variety. The points—mask, ears, legs, feet, and tail—must be all of the same shade and clearly defined. The mask should cover the entire face including the whisker pads and be connected to the ears by traced markings. There should be no ticking or white hairs in the points.

Coloring The body color is bluish-white of a glacial tone; the points color blue-gray. The nose leather and paw pads are blue-gray. The eye color is deep, vivid blue.

Build Medium-sized, long, slim, and athletic, with a long, flat-profiled, wedge-shaped head and large, wide-set ears.

Temperament Lively, intelligent, and inquisitive; demands attention and has a loud voice.

Chocolate Point Siamese

Although the original Royal Cats of Siam were seal-pointed, some had lighter brown points, and these were eventually recognized as being a separate color variety, which was called Chocolate Point, the first of which was recorded in 1931. The fur of the Siamese is short, very soft, and exceedingly fine, and daily brushing with a medium-hard brush to remove dead hairs is recommended, especially during shedding periods. A diet that includes fish and cooked vegetables used alternately with meat will help maintain coat color.

Coloring The body color is ivory; the points color is milk chocolate. The nose leather is milk chocolate; the paw pads are cinnamon to milk chocolate. The eye color is deep, vivid blue.

Build Medium-sized, long, slim, and athletic, with a long, flat-profiled, wedge-shaped head and large, wide-set ears.

Temperament Lively, intelligent, and inquisitive; demands attention.

Cream Point Siamese

It was inevitable that once the Red Point Siamese was established, its natural dilution, the paler-colored Cream Point, would follow.

In exhibition, the Siamese is penalized for having belly spots or spots on the flanks. It will also lose points for white or lighter-colored hairs or ticked hairs in the points.

Coloring The body color is creamy white; the points are pastel cream. The nose leather and paw pads are pink. The eye color is deep, vivid blue.

Build Medium-sized, long, slim, and athletic, with a long, flat-profiled, wedge-shaped head and large, wide-set ears.

Temperament Lively, intelligent, and inquisitive; demands attention and has a loud voice.

Lilac Point Siamese

The Lilac Point, which is also known as the Frost Point in some of the cat associations, is the palest of the Siamese.

Once Blue and Chocolate Point cats were being bred, it is quite likely that the Lilac Points occurred naturally, but it was the introduction of the Russian Blue to the Siamese line in the late 1940s that set this color form on a firm footing.

Coloring The body color is glacial white (magnolia); the points are a frosty gray with a slight pinkish tone. The nose leather and paw pads are lavender-pink. The eye color is deep, vivid blue.

Build Medium-sized, long, slim, and athletic, with a long, flat-profiled, wedge-shaped head and large, wide-set ears.

Temperament Lively, intelligent, and inquisitive; demands attention and has a loud voice.

Red Point Siamese

This is a cat of extreme show type, with its large flared ears following the lines of the wedge-shaped head. The body is creamy white, and the matching points are a warm orange.

The short fine coat is kept in good condition by stroking with clean hands or buffing with a silk scarf. The large ears need regular cleaning, and Siamese should be provided with a scratching post and lots of toys.

Coloring The body color is creamy white; the points color is bright, warm orange. The nose leather is pink; paw pads are pink and/or red. The eye color is deep, vivid blue.

Build Medium-sized, long, slim, and athletic, with a long, flat-profiled, wedge-shaped head and large, wide-set ears.

Temperament Lively, intelligent, and inquisitive; demands attention and has a loud voice.

Seal Point Siamese

With its distinctively colored points set against a pale background, the Seal Point is probably the best known of all pedigree breeds.

The typical Siamese cat has an extrovert personality. It is very affectionate with people and pets that it likes, is lively and intelligent, and can be very vocal. Siamese cats do not like being left alone for long periods, and do better as pets when kept in pairs or small groups. They are naturally fastidiously clean and make perfect house pets.

Coloring The body color is beige to cream or pale fawn; the points color dark seal brown. The nose leather and paw pads are dark seal brown; the eye color is deep, vivid blue.

Build Medium-sized, long, slim, and athletic, with a long, flat-profiled, wedge-shaped head and large, wide-set ears.

Temperament Lively, intelligent, and inquisitive; demands attention and has a loud voice.

Blue Tabby Point Siamese

Originally known as Shadow Points and sometimes called Lynx Points, Tabby Point Siamese were first recorded as early as 1902. It was not, however, until 1961 that a litter of Tabby Points was shown, and it created quite a stir.

Coloring The body color is bluish-white; the points are blue-gray tabby. The rims around the eyes and nose are blue-gray. The nose leather is old rose or blue-gray; the paw pads are blue-gray. The eye color is deep, vivid blue.

Build Medium-sized, long, slim, and athletic, with a long, flat-profiled, wedge-shaped head and large, wide-set ears.
Temperament Lively, intelligent, and inquisitive; demands attention and has a loud voice.

Red Tabby Point Siamese

The personality of all Siamese can be subject to wide, unpredictable mood swings. One day it will be a happy, playful cat; the next day it will be a moody, sulking one. The Siamese can also be quite jealous of other cats and even of other humans. It is one of the few cat breeds that can be trained to walk on a leash like a dog.

Coloring The body color is off-white with a slight red tinge; the points are warm orange tabby. The rims around the eyes and nose are dark pink. The nose leather is old brick red or pink; the paw pads are pink. The eye color is deep, vivid blue.

Build Medium-sized, long, slim, and athletic, with a long, flat-profiled, wedge-shaped head and large, wide-set ears.
Temperament Lively, intelligent, and inquisitive; demands attention and has a loud voice.

Tortoiseshell Point Siamese

Tortoiseshell cats are usually a female-only variety, with the occasional resulting male proving to be sterile. Tortoiseshell (or Tortie) Point Siamese are no exception. Popular in its own right, the Tortoiseshell Point is instrumental in breeding programs for Red and Cream Point Siamese.

In common with other Siamese, the body must be even in color, with only subtle shading. The points— mask, ears, legs, feet, and tail—must be all of the same shade and clearly defined. The mask should cover the entire face, including the whisker pads, and be connected to the ears by traced marking.

Coloring The body color is ivory; the points are milk chocolate, patched or mingled with red and/or light red. The nose leather is milk chocolate and/or pink; paw pads are cinnamon to milk chocolate and/or pink. The eye color is deep, vivid blue.

Build Medium-sized, long, slim, and athletic, with a long, flat-profiled, wedge-shaped head and large, wide-set ears.

Temperament Lively, intelligent, and inquisitive; demands attention and has a loud voice.

Tiffanie

The Tiffanie breed combines the conformation and coloring of the typical Burmese with an attractive coat of long silky hair. First developed in the United States from longcoated kittens, which appeared from time to time in otherwise normal litters of pedigree Burmese, the Tiffanie was later developed as a breed in its own right. The American breeders concentrated on the sable Tiffanie, born a pale *café au lait* color, and gradually developing the long sable coat with maturity. In Britain, longcoated cats of good Burmese conformation came from the Burmilla breeding programs and were refined by back-crosses to Burmese, which resulted in Tiffanie kittens of all colors found in the Burmese and Malayan ranges.

Just like its Burmese ancestors, the Tiffanie is playful and affectionate with an extrovert nature, making it a good pet.

The long coat is quite easy to care for with regular grooming.

Coloring Blue, chocolate, lilac, caramel, red, cream, apricot, and associated tortoiseshells. It is accepted in silver and standard version, and in full Burmese range. It may also be shaded, smoke, tabby, or black self-color.

Build Medium-sized and surprisingly heavy for its size.

Temperament Outgoing, friendly, sociable, and athletic.

Tonkinese

A hybrid of Burmese and Siamese cats, the Tonkinese has physical features of both these breeds. A mating between a Burmese and a Siamese gives all Tonkinese kittens, whereas the mating of two Tonkinese cats produces, on average, two Tonkinese kittens to one Burmese and one Siamese.

Tonkinese cats have dark points which merge gradually into the body color, which is intermediate between the typical pale Siamese and the dark Burmese coloring. Tonkinese eye color is blue-green or turquoise, never Siamese blue or Burmese gold.

The Tonkinese is a friendly and affectionate cat, with a strong sense of mischief.

The coat is very easy to keep in good condition with very little grooming. Regular combing to remove dead hair, and buffing with a silk scarf or grooming mitten imparts a healthy sheen.

Coloring Natural mink, brown (shown here), blue, champagne, platinum mink, red, cream, torbie, blue torbie, champagne mink torbie, platinum mink torbie. In all forms, eye color is blue-green.

Build Medium-sized, muscular, and surprisingly heavy for its size.

Temperament Friendly, affectionate, mischievous, and intelligent; a good family pet, getting on well with other cats as well as with dogs and children.

Red Mink Tonkinese

The Tonkinese is bred from Burmese and Siamese and, as would be expected, is intermediate to those breeds in both conformation and coloring. As a pet it suits those people who find the show-type Siamese to be too extreme, but do not favor the typical chunkiness and almost uniform coloration of the Burmese. Indeed, a typical Tonkinese is very similar to the "old-fashioned" type of Siamese cat that many people today desire as pets.

Coloring The golden-cream coat has apricot underparts. The points are light to medium ruddy brown; the nose leather and paw pads are caramel-pink. The eye color is blue-green.

Build Medium-sized, muscular, and surprisingly heavy for its size.

Temperament Friendly, affectionate, mischievous, and intelligent; a good family pet, getting on well with other cats as well as with dogs and children.

Chocolate Pointed Tonkinese

The "points" are the mask (face) ears, legs and paws, and the tail. The points are densely marked, but gradually merge into the body color. The color of the points is the same as the body color, but denser and darker.

Allowance is made for the lighter body color in kittens and adolescent cats, and for slight barring in the coat; colors darken with maturity— full coloration may take up to 16 months to develop, particularly in the dilute color varieties.

Coloring The body color in the adult cat should be rich and even, and shade almost imperceptibly into a slightly lighter color on the underparts. There is a distinct contrast between the points and body color whatever the color variety. The eye color is blue-green (aquamarine), with depth, clarity and brilliance.

Build Medium-sized, muscular, and surprisingly heavy for its size.

Temperament Friendly, affectionate, mischievous, and intelligent; a good family pet, getting on well with other cats as well as with dogs and children.

BREEDING

Although ordinary domestic cats seem to become pregnant and produce kittens without much bother—often against their owners' wishes—the production of pedigree kittens under controlled conditions can prove difficult, and cat breeding should not be undertaken lightly.

Despite its many generations of domestication, a cat can resent the unnatural restrictions placed upon her during mating and pregnancy. She may prove unwilling to mate with the stud cat chosen for her; she may have a stressful gestation period or a difficult delivery. She could reject her kittens, have little or poor-quality milk, or be so unsettled that she spends her time anxiously moving the kittens to new nest sites.

A successful cat breeder will be someone for whom financial gain is not important. Breeding pedigree cats is a hobby full of rewards, but none of these is financial. There is a great sense of pride and achievement in planning a special litter, seeing it born, and rearing it. A true cat lover will gain a great deal from caring for the female cat, known as the brood queen, helping her through the weeks of pregnancy, attending the birth, and looking after the needs of the growing family. On the debit side is the problem of parting with the kittens when they are fully independent and ready to go to new homes, which will be when they are about three months old.

It may seem logical to buy a pair of cats in order to start breeding, but this is impractical. Keeping a stud male is not a job for the novice. He will not be content with a monogamous relationship with one queen and will need special accommodation of his own, so that his habit of spray-marking his territory with strong-smelling urine does not become a serious household problem.

Oriental cats, such as the Siamese, often have more than the average number of kittens in a litter and need extra care in order to rear them successfully. This superb seal point has eight strong and healthy youngsters.

To start breeding it is best to buy one or two females of the breed you have chosen, seeking advice from an experienced breeder or show judge, and purchasing the very best females you can afford. Two females will keep each other company, and, if they are unrelated, they will provide you with a good foundation to lines of your own in future years. A kitten for breeding should be purchased when about three months old. She should be of sound conformation, with a good temperament and an impeccable pedigree, and should be properly registered with an acceptable cat association. She should be well grown for her age and should have received a suitable course of vaccinations, for which you will be provided with certificates. Until she grows to adulthood, the kitten should lead a normal life, with good food, correct grooming, and lots of play opportunities combined with tender loving care.

Kittens vary as to when they have their first season or period of estrus, so she must be carefully observed and not allowed to roam free. When her first season occurs, she should be carefully watched. At the next period of estrus, if she is at least ten months of age, it is feasible for her to be mated if your veterinary surgeon agrees that she is well enough and physically fit.

Pedigree male cats kept for breeding are called stud cats. They have usually proved their superior qualities in the show ring, attaining high show status because they conform so closely to the standard of points for their respective breeds. Because a working stud male will habitually spray his habitat with spurts of pungent urine as territorial marking behavior, he has to be confined in his own living quarters.

Matings must be strictly controlled, witnessed, and recorded by the stud's owner, who will issue a breeding certificate to the queen's owner, who pays an agreed stud fee. The two cats are given some hours to become accustomed to one another, and once the stud's owner is assured that the cats

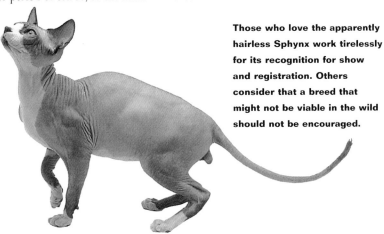

Those who love the apparently hairless Sphynx work tirelessly for its recognition for show and registration. Others consider that a breed that might not be viable in the wild should not be encouraged.

SELECTIVE BREEDING

From time to time, anomalies occur in litters of kittens, in both pedigrees and domestics and, quite often, breeders who are fascinated by all things new or unusual may decide to try to perpetuate the unusual features and perhaps produce a new breed. It is possible, after selectively breeding one or several generations, to determine the genetic make-up of a new feline feature, and then to set out a formal and constructive breeding program to develop a new breed. Some features which are clearly detrimental to a cat's well-being would be frowned upon by true cat lovers and would thus prove unacceptable to most associations for registration and breeding purposes.

The curled ears of the American Curl do not appear to present any problems, and the breed is accepted by some associations in the United States.

are relating and not aggressive, and that the queen is really ready, she is released from the pen and the cats are allowed to mate. This procedure is repeated, usually over two or three days, to make sure that a completely successful mating has taken place, then the queen is returned to her owner.

The Scottish Fold is refused recognition by some associations on the premise that the tightly folded ears are impossible to keep clean and healthy, and because some skeletal anomalies were apparent in some early kittens.

MATERNITY

Feline mothers care for their kittens in a wholly dedicated way until the kittens are able to take care of their own needs. Male cats are not involved in the rearing of kittens, although they have been observed playing with kittens in feral cat colonies.

After mating, the fertilized ova become implanted in the uterine wall of the female cat, and glands secrete hormones, giving rise to certain patterns of behavior. The cat becomes even more sensitive to danger, she grooms herself even more thoroughly than before, and her appetite gradually increases. If she is a free-roaming cat, she will hunt with more dedication, and she will also nibble selected grasses and herbage.

As her pregnancy advances, the cat chooses secluded sleeping areas. Her self-grooming sessions increase, and she pays

The mother cat constantly grooms her kittens, washing them by licking them all over with her rough tongue.

particular attention to her genital area and gradually enlarging breasts. As the period of gestation of about 63 days reaches its end, the cat searches for a suitable site in which to give birth. The first stage of labor can extend for many hours. The cat is restless and will not eat, although she will drink from time to time. Eventually, when the second stage of labor commences, with typical contractions, the cat will generally go to the place she has chosen to give birth. The contractions gradually become stronger and more frequent, and prior to the expulsion of the first kitten, a sac of fluid may be passed, preparing the passage for the birth.

Kittens may be born head first or tail first, both presentations being equally normal. The head or rump appears, and the cat licks at the membranes as contractions push the tiny kitten out. Sometimes,

Kittens are born blind and deaf, but have a strong sense of smell, which enables them to find a nipple and to start feeding even before they are perfectly dry.

particularly with the first-born, the kitten seems to be held back by its shoulders or hips, but it is normally expelled without human interference as the cat shifts her position and bears down. She licks away all the membranes encasing the newly born kittens and chews the umbilical cord to within about half an inch of the kitten's body. The stump of cord dries and drops off, leaving a neat navel within about a week. The placenta may be passed still attached to the kitten, or may be expelled later, after the kitten is clean, dry, and nursing. The mother cat will normally eat the placenta, which is rich in nutrients, and which, in the wild, would sustain her until she was fit enough to hunt for food.

After the birth of the first kitten, the rest of the litter follow at regular intervals, and the mother cat deals with each in the same way. She licks and washes each kitten, clearing the membrane from its body,

Over the years, cats have been selectively bred to conform to standards of point laid down by various cat associations. Here we see the extremes in type between the svelte, long-headed Oriental (left) and the heavy, round-headed Persian (below).

A mother cat may decide to move her litter to a new nest, and she will carry the kittens one at a time, holding them firmly by the scruff of the neck.

cleaning the mucus from its nose and mouth, and stimulating it to breathe. She also licks vigorously at the kitten's anal region, stimulating the tiny animal to pass meconium, a dark plug which stops up its bowel until released.

When the last kitten of the litter has been born, the mother cat washes her own genital region, legs, and tail. She gathers her kittens together and lying on one side, encourages them to suckle. She may not leave the nest for up to 24 hours for food and a drink. Young kittens urinate and defecate only when stimulated to do so by the mother cat. She has a set routine for kitten care. After nursing the kittens, she washes and grooms them in turn, and swallows all the excreted material they produce, to make sure that the nest remains clean. This would be a safety factor in the wild, preventing scent-leaving clues as to the kittens' whereabouts.

Even after centuries of domestication, cats often revert to the innate behavior patterns of their wild ancestors. Three weeks or so after the birth of her litter, the cat may suddenly decide to move the kittens to another, often quite unsuitable, location. She grasps each kitten around the neck, holding it in her jaws, but not piercing the skin with her teeth, lifts the kitten by raising her head, and carries it between her straddled forelegs to its new resting place. The cat will carry each kitten in turn until she is satisfied that the litter is in a new, safe haven. When kittens are grasped around the neck, their natural response is to assume the fetal position and go completely limp. This means that they are rarely harmed by being carried.

Until the kittens are about three weeks old, the mother cat looks after all their needs, leaving only to eat, drink, and relieve herself, and returning as quickly as possible to her babies. By ten days, the kittens have opened their eyes and gradually begin to respond to various stimulae. During their third and fourth weeks, they try to leave the nest area, become stronger and more mobile, and gradually accept solid food, spending less time with the mother.

During their early weeks of life, their mother teaches the kittens a great deal about being feline. She encourages play behavior,

including mock hunting and killing moves, and she initiates the first stages in toilet training, calling them to follow her away from the nest when they want to urinate and defecate. By the time the kittens are weaned and ready to go to new homes, their mother will have made sure that each is an independent and self-assured little cat.

DEVELOPMENT OF KITTENS

Kittens are born blind and deaf. They have a strong sense of smell, however, which enables them to locate their mother's nipples, and a strong sucking reflex, which means that they take in enough milk to satisfy their needs. About one week to ten days after birth, the eyes open and the hearing starts to develop, and until the litter is three weeks old, the queen looks after the kittens constantly, feeding and grooming, stimulating them to urinate and defecate by licking at their genital regions. The queen ingests the kittens' wastes and spends about 70 percent of her time attending to her family.

At two weeks, the kittens can scramble around their nest box and at three weeks start to stand up on their legs and pay attention to what is going on around them. Between three and six weeks, they make great advances, learning to play, to make sounds, and show an interest in solid food. From about four weeks, they will use a corner of their box for toilet purposes and by six weeks can be taught to use a litter tray. Having learned to eat a variety of foods and spent time away from mother, kittens are independent by eight to ten weeks.

SHOWING

People who breed or show cats are called cat fanciers, and they usually take up the hobby through an all-consuming love of all things feline.

Cat fanciers share a common bond and interest in wanting to breed or own the perfect cat. Most cats show complete indifference to being put on public display, but owners derive great personal satisfaction in gaining top awards with their pets.

There is little financial reward for the successful exhibitor; entry fees are high and prize money is often non-existent. Rosettes, ribbons, and trophies are eagerly sought after, and proudly displayed at home. Exhibitors enjoy cat shows as regular social functions. All members of the family are able to attend and enjoy the proceedings, and some cats actually appear to enjoy being pampered and admired by judges and the receptive audience of the show hall.

The first cat show ever recorded was held in 1598 at St. Giles Fair in Winchester, England, but the first properly benched show, with cats being placed in individual cages, took place at London's Crystal Palace in 1871. The first benched American cat show was held in Madison Square Garden,

Although there is no monetary gain in showing cats, the winning of first-place awards is the aim of most exhibitors. Here a lovely Chinchilla neuter and a kitten pose with their awards.

New York, in 1895. The vogue for exhibiting cats and competing for prizes spread slowly around the world, and today hundreds of shows take place in many different countries. Each country with an active band of cat fanciers has one or more governing bodies, and they accept cats for registration and promote the running of licensed cat shows.

Each registering body has its own rules and guidelines for breeding, registration, and showing cats, and often publishes useful information on all aspects of cat care, breeding, and exhibiting. In North America, cat lovers have a wide choice of cat organizations from which to choose.

The best way to enter the world of showing is to start by reading one of the many specialist cat magazines that are available. Shows are listed, and a day or two watching the proceedings can be invaluable. Most exhibitors are more than delighted to talk about their cats, and about show

procedures. All shows have information desks with helpful assistants, and once you become a member of an association you have access to a vast wealth of data. Each association has its own rules and methods of show organization, but in one aspect they are all identical—the cat's welfare is the first priority at all times.

Show procedures vary, but the end result is the same. Cats are assessed by qualified judges who relate each cat's qualities to an official standard of points for its breed or variety, and then rank each cat in a class in order of merit. Various groups have their own nomenclature for top award-winning cats—Champion, Supreme Champion, and so on. Even non-pedigree domestic cats may be shown and have a special section at most shows. As they cannot be assessed against any breed standard, they are judged on temperament, condition, and their overall esthetic appeal.

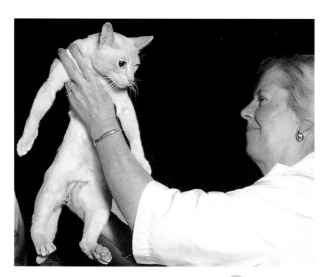

At GCCF shows, cats are individually judged at their show pens after the exhibitors have been asked to vacate the main body of the show hall.

FELINE ASSOCIATIONS AND GOVERNING BODIES

Countries where pedigree cats are bred and exhibited have one or more associations or governing bodies that keep a register of cats and their lineage and that set down rules and regulations for cat shows. Britain has the Governing Council of the Cat Fancy (GCCF) and the Cat Association of Britain, which is the British member of FIFe. American cat fanciers have several associations, the largest being the Cat Fancier's Association (CFA), which also has affiliated clubs in Canada and Japan.

In Europe, Australasia, and South Africa, there are national bodies and other associations, and generally one in each country is a member of the Federation Internationale Feline (FiFe), which is the largest and most powerful of the feline associations in the world. FiFe has thousands of members, covering the entire world of cats, and trains and licences judges of high caliber throughout the world.

United States

American Association of Cat Enthusiasts, P.O. Box 213, Pine Brook, New Jersey 07058. Tel: (973) 335 6717; Fax: (973) 334 5834.

ACA America's oldest cat registry, having been active since 1899, the **American Cat Association** is a fairly small association, which holds shows in the southeast and southwest of the United States. American Cat Association (ACA), 8101 Katherine Drive, Panorama City, CA 91402.

ACC Based in the southwest, the **American Cat Council** is a small association, which has modified "English-style" shows in which exhibitors must vacate the show hall during judging.

CCFF Although it is one of the smaller associations in the United States, the **Crown Cat Fanciers' Federation** has many shows each year in the northeast and southeastern regions, and also in western Canada.

CFA The **Cat Fanciers' Association** is the largest US association, incorporated and run by a board of directors. It produces an impressive annual yearbook full of articles, breeders' advertisements, and beautiful color photographs. There is a CFA show held somewhere in the United States almost every weekend of the year. Cat Fanciers' Association Inc., (CFA Inc), P.O. Box 1005, Manasquan, New Jersey 08736 0805. Tel: (732) 528 9797; Fax: (732) 528 7391.

CFF With its many activities centered in the northeastern region of the United States, the **Cat Fanciers' Federation** is a registering body of medium size. Cat Fanciers' Federation (CFF), 9509 Montgomery Road, Cincinnati OH 45242. e.mail address: http://www.cffinc.org

UCF A medium-sized association, the **United Cat Federation** is centered in the southwest of the United States.

Worldwide

ACFA An international association and run very democratically, the **American Cat Fanciers' Association** has affiliated clubs in Canada and Japan, and produces a monthly news bulletin for members.

FIFe Most European countries have at least two bodies for the registration of cats, and licensing of shows. One body is almost certain to be affiliated to the **Federation Internationale Feline**, an enormous and well-organized incorporated and chartered society which also has affiliates in countries

beyond Europe. Fully established in 1949, FIFe is today the largest cat body in the world, uniting more than 150,000 breeders and exhibitors in the world of show cats.

TICA The International Cat Association produces a bi-monthly newsletter and a yearbook. It has a modern approach to showing and has shows throughout the United States and affiliates in Canada and Japan. International Cat Association, P.O. Box 2684, Harlingen, Texas 78551.